NARCISSISTIC MOTHERS AND COVERT EMOTIONAL ABUSE

For Adult Children of Narcissistic Parents

By Diana Macey

Table of Contents

PREFIX 3

PART I: Covert Narcissistic Mothers and Small Children....................14
PART II: Covert Narcissistic Mothers and Children............................44
PART III: Covert Narcissistic Mothers and Teenagers........................84
PART IV: Narcissists and Adult Children...112
PART V: Recovery..131

WHO THIS BOOK IS FOR

Have you ever had the following experience: Someone, a new acquaintance or a colleague, is being nice to you because they like you, and you try so hard to justify their faith in you that you end up doing exactly the opposite? You were unable to handle being liked gracefully and ended angry and disappointed with yourself. Somehow a good thing turned into an unpleasant and emotionally draining experience.

You are not alone.

This book is for adults who don't know why they find themselves struggling with the things in life that come naturally to others, who can't find joy even when there is not much obviously wrong with their lives. It's for those who find socialising draining because they are easily affected by the moods and the words of others and cannot understand why sadness and dissatisfaction prevail in their lives while others thrive with seemingly a lot less.

This book is for adults who suspect something was wrong with their childhood, but are unable to express why it felt so bad without being able to point to any of the horrific abuse often talked about in the media.

If you struggle with such issues you might be an adult child of a covert narcissistic parent.

Other signs of such abuse are chronic anxiety, getting overwhelmed, concentration problems, substance abuse, irritability, flashbacks of humiliating moments from the past, inability to cope with failure and negative emotions, and inability to accept compliments and enjoy the simple things others enjoy.

This indicates something is fundamentally wrong with your mental state, and it is the result of the prolonged abuse you've been through. Worst of all, the abuse is not easily visible or widely acknowledged, and you don't know how to begin to heal.

Understanding the problem will help you start recovering.

And, of course, this book is for those who already know about narcissism and narcissistic abuse. More specifically it's about covert narcissistic mothers, and how they inflict lasting damage on their children.

WHO I AM AND WHY I WROTE THIS BOOK

I am an adult survivor of childhood emotional abuse. It took me years of struggling with depression and all of the issues I mentioned above to finally stumble across information about covert narcissism and dysfunctional family dynamics.

Understanding what happened to me, what the damage was and where it came from, helped me heal and improve my state of mind.

After my last severe breakdown I researched the topics of childhood emotional abuse, dysfunctional families, cluster B personality disorders, and emotional neglect. I found I was not alone, and there was a way of shifting my mindset and improving my mental health.

I am very thankful to those who made the effort to write and talk about their experiences. There is a lot of good information out there, but I could not find enough examples of real situations to illustrate the narcissistic behaviour patterns.

This is why I decided to write this book. It has many memories from my early childhood through to the recovery stage in my 40s. I will try to pass on the knowledge I gained from many different sources, and hopefully it will be helpful to you and your recovery.

I am not a medical professional and I haven't studied the topic academically. I have learned from acclaimed academic sources, as well as from bloggers and adult children of narcissistic parents sharing their knowledge online.

I am using the terminology used in the online community. It instantly resonated with me and my experiences when I first started reading about narcissism and covert narcissists. I will try to summarise what I've learned and illustrate it with examples from my experience with my covert narcissistic mother and dysfunctional family of origin.

For those who are new to the topic I will begin with a brief summary.

COVERT NARCISSISTIC ABUSE

Covert narcissistic parents break down their children's self-esteem and sense of self in order to manipulate them into serving their needs. The abuse is subtle and, over time, it erodes the victim's personality, distorts their sense of reality, and it causes severe damage to their ability to function in their day-to-day lives.

And if you wonder why anyone would do that, the answer is simple: the narcissists are not mentally healthy people and their goal is not to raise mentally healthy offspring.

Most parents do not destroy their child. Narcissism is classified as a personality disorder for a reason, and it has to do with the predatory and inadequate way of sustaining the narcissistic ego. It is classified as a cluster B personality disorder with a specific set of dynamics and outcomes.

This book is not about the academic description; your parents might've had a full-blown narcissism or had strong tendencies, either way their unhealthy behaviour affected you and you need to understand what happened to you in order to heal.

Covert narcissists are different from the rest of their kind because they are vulnerable to stress and worry, but that does not make them less dangerous. Their goals are achieved with tricky head games and manipulation techniques, and by instilling huge amounts of toxic shame and guilt into their children.

WHY COVERT NARCISSISTIC PARENTS ABUSE

Probably because of some early childhood trauma, lack of control, or being idealised, the false image was created to replace the authentic self – the image of someone special and deserving, someone who cannot be faulted or shamed.

This false image needs to be constantly maintained because the validation comes from outside interactions, and the narcissists cannot sustain it on their own merits. This is why everyone around them must be made to preserve the false image and make the narcissists feel good about themselves.

This is a dysfunctional and energy consuming way to be. And if you look behind the smoke and mirrors of the false image they project, the narcissists are very dysfunctional people. They need a constant supply of validation and reassurance.

This is why the narcissists have children – to get a lifetime supply of adoration and control as the higher power in the relationship. They expect that the children should somehow fix what is wrong with their lives, bring happiness and fulfilment, and validate their special status in life. This is a tall order for a child. This is why the narcissistic abuse is so damaging and consuming – it defies reason and logic. It is a game of shame and blame, of twisting reality to benefit the parent.

The narcissistic parents lack empathy, and that is the ability to place themselves in the position of the children, to feel what they feel and react in a constructive manner that will benefit the development of the child. What they want and need is someone to reflect back to them the false image they have created, to maintain it and project it to others.

What they want from their children is narcissistic supply.

WHAT IS NARCISSISTIC SUPPLY

Narcissistic supply is exactly that – being seen as a superior, a higher authority, a special, capable, wiser and faultless person, and being held in higher esteem than the rest. If it is pointed out that they are not that, then the narcissists react with childish rage. Being acknowledged, having their superior image confirmed and reflected by others, is the drug they need. This is why control is very important. Being in control means they are the ones that are better and special, and they tell others what is right and wrong.

The narcissists want the same from all people, but they are in a position of power and it is much easier for them to manipulate their children. As the children grow up and try to develop their own personalities, the narcissistic parent has to implement a wide range of techniques to keep on getting supply.

Ultimately, the fact that the narcissists are damaged and dysfunctional means they have to damage those around them even more to keep control.

THE GAP BETWEEN THE FALSE IMAGE AND THE REALITY

There is a big problem with having to maintain a false image, of course. The narcissists are not the superior beings they think they are. To maintain that false self that constantly clashes with the reality, they have to be masters of manipulation. They develop complex ways to blame others when things don't go their way, while still projecting a good image to anyone who will buy it. Their existence is based on keeping their false image, and their offspring is burdened with the task of filling the gap between image and reality and paying the price with their own mental health and wellbeing.

THEIR VICTIMS

What you have to understand as a victim of narcissistic parents, is that they had to make you feel inadequate because they could not manipulate mentally healthy, self-reliant, and resilient offspring. To make you serve their needs they had to break your personality, your borders, and your good sense.

Their methods are manipulation, projection, gaslighting, devaluation, triangulation, refusal to take responsibility, undermining, smear campaigns, shaming, twisting your thoughts and feelings, negativity, humiliation disguised as jokes, and so on.

The attacks on the self-esteem are meant to destroy the children's independence and strength, to make them deny their own needs, serve the narcissistic parent and accept their version of reality. They need that because the projected image is not authentic and has to be acknowledged and mirrored by outside sources. This is why maintaining the image takes so much effort on the part of the narcissist.

Not everyone can be a source of supply and a target of narcissistic abuse. Covert narcissists are not a big threat to mentally healthy people because such people sense something is wrong and would not let the narcissist exploit them. This is why covert narcissists surround themselves with dysfunction, choose someone they can manipulate for a spouse, and inflict narcissistic wounds they can exploit on their children.

WHY THE ABUSE IS HIDDEN

Covert narcissists are different than other abusers because they purposefully project a good image of themselves to the outside world. They want to be seen as what society would refer to as 'good people.'

It is a part of the illusion for the covert narcissists. To make the false image work they need you to play along, to enable them, to project back the false image. They become openly abusive only when their manipulation techniques fail to work.

Narcissists prey on your empathy and willing servitude because they have to count on your good nature for the ability to shame you and to make you empathise with their problems.

This is why they claim the high moral ground, always pretend to be the victim, and accuse their children of being bad if they do not respond the way they want them to.

Covert narcissists prey on people with the right weaknesses for them to exploit. This is why the abuse is wrapped in a pretence of care, and they can get people fooled for a very long time.

THE REAL NARCISSISTS

The covert narcissists are chronic abusers who project an image that is outwardly holy and good, when in fact they are anything but. Only those close to them get to see the real narcissist: entitled and self-absorbed, smug when you are in trouble, always ready to kick you when you are down, to criticise and demean you. Covert narcissists are passive-aggressive, manipulative, exploitive, and always claiming to be the victim.

The narcissistic image is static and not likely to change. In the heart of it is feeling special and privileged for no reason, and having a lot of rage against anything challenging that image.

The worst thing about covert narcissists is that they can get away with the abuse of their children for a very long time, even when the children are adults and have families of their own. The abuse is hidden and subtle, so they cannot be confronted about one thing. It is a lifelong, abusive pattern of behaviour. Once the victims figure that out, however, the narcissists lose their power.

This is why it is a personality disorder. The narcissists are bound to it; they get hurt by it as well, but are unable to change. Unfortunately, because they don't know where to stop, they often destroy their children so badly they can no longer function enough to serve anybody's needs.

This enrages the narcissists and instead of helping they watch their victims suffer and unravel with sick pleasure and make the situation worse. This is why they are so dangerous – they build an image of a good person, but they have no empathy or humanity. This is the sickness, the double bind that breaks the victims.

If you are an adult child of a narcissist you know they do nothing to help when you are falling apart, take pleasure in your suffering, and then claim they are the true victims and you are 'bad' for failing to please them after they've done everything for you.

Covert narcissism is the ultimate abuse of the word 'good.' They must be seen as 'good people,' you must be a 'good child' to serve them. To be 'good' in the narcissistic world, you have to betray your own feelings and needs. You have to agree they are great when they are not, that they are right when they are not.

Narcissists won't take responsibility for their shortcoming in the context of the normal human experience, so they project what they don't like about themselves onto others. This is why their kids suffer. The image that is mirrored to them by the parent is distorted through the personality disorder and does not serve the well-being of the children.

WHAT HAPPENS TO THE CHILDREN

Children of covert narcissists have very little chance of growing up as healthy individuals. This is why mental disorders pass on from generation to generation. The truth of the matter is that parents who are mentally ill cannot teach their children good mental health. Their reason for having children in the first place is to have a lifetime supply of external validation to feed their fake and misplaced egos. They get power and control that is inbuilt into the family system.

The unspoken message they send to the children is 'I gave you life, you owe me, you will be who I want you to be and you will make me feel good.' The parents take their children's love, loyalty, and validation but give none of it back.

A devastating outcome of the narcissistic abuse is that their children end up treating themselves in the same abusive way. The harsh and nasty inner voice they have is a direct result of the narcissistic abuse.

THE CYCLE OF ABUSE

'The best memories I have are from the time you were little' – this is a sentiment expressed by many narcissistic mothers, including mine. She was angrily and bitterly disappointed by the adult version of me and my episodes of crippling depression. 'I hope our grandchildren will turn out to be better,' she used to tell relatives as if I wasn't even there. My mother was openly disgusted and disappointed by me and she was waiting for grandchildren to relive the past good times.

This is a pattern many children of narcissists will recognise. The narcissistic mother manages to suck the life out of her children and she needs new sources of supply. Small children are the best; they are excellent source of narcissistic supply. They are easy to control, and have no defences against the narcissistic manipulations.

My mother had a plan to get the validation she needed from her obedient and 'good' offspring. That is not how things turned out for her. With time, the narcissists become more needy and more reckless, and because they do not have the ability to create good relationships they end up alone. Regardless, during their lifetime they manage to use and abuse many people, especially their kids.

PART I: Covert Narcissistic Mothers and Small Children

Covert narcissists are nicer to their children when they are small, and this is when they do the worst damage to them. Young brains are most receptive to suggestions and the narcissists can uphold their false image and appear to be good parents.

For a very long time if someone asked me 'What was your childhood like,' I would've said 'fine.' Abuse, to my limited knowledge, was beating and starving children. On the surface mine was a typical middle-class family – we had food, shelter, and clothes. My brother and I were looked after; we had cooked food, we went to bed on time, and got praised for good behaviour. On the surface we were good children, very well behaved, if not a little too shy in social situations.

My father was working most of the time. He didn't seem to know what to say and he wasn't easy to be around. My mother, on the other hand, was very contented as a mother, and she cherished and promoted her status in the family. She was in her element, and I remember her saying things like 'mothers love their children,' and 'nobody will love you like your family' to me on many occasions. Children, in her words, were supposed to 'be the joy in the lives of their parents.'

As a kid I loved and idolised her with the neediness of a small child. I wanted to be with her at all times. My mother liked being with us, she made meals and took us to the park and used to talk a lot which made it easy to be around her.

Mothers are very important to small children. My mother definitely was, and she would often tell me what a good mother she was. For example, she told me that she breastfed me for six months, and that some mothers give formula to their babies instead. Such mothers were held in contempt by her. 'There are some really bad mothers out there,' she used to say with dramatic outrage in her voice. I listened to each and every word, and in my mind she was a good mother.

Indeed, being a mother was something she was proud of. She told me that women who do not want to have children are selfish. I assumed that was because having kids was so hard on a woman. 'The pregnancies took all the calcium from my teeth,' she said when explaining to me why she had to go to the dentist. It made me feel responsible, as well as the usual 'everything we do is for you.' I felt bad they had to work so hard to buy food and clothes for me, and I felt I had to justify my existence and repay them somehow.

My mother had a favourite story about me crying for her so loudly she could hear me from way down the street. 'You were screaming as if someone was killing you, and your grandmother didn't know what to do …' I could remember crying, and the deep desperation and dread I was feeling. I was experiencing sheer terror from my head to my toes, my stomach convulsing with the fear my mummy would never come back. She was the single most important person to me. As a small child I loved her to bits, she was the centre of my world, the one person I depended on and naturally I wanted to please her.

'It makes me feel good when people tell me how well you behave …,' she used to say. When she was upset with me she used to threaten me with 'You are going to make me sick, and I am going to die, and what are you going to do then?'

I had no idea what I was going to do and I felt worried when she was upset or angry, or my father was upset or angry. Each time they walked through the door I was searching for signs of tiredness and bad mood. My father always had them and I never felt comfortable around him. My mother … not often, but when she did my heart used to sink down to my stomach.

WHAT IS EMOTIONAL INCEST?

That was the way I was raised and I had nothing else to compare it with. I got to read about it as an adult; in the academic literature, making children responsible for the emotional well-being of the parents was referred to as emotional incest. It is a heavy burden for young children because they do not even know how to look after their own emotions yet.

Kids cannot understand when the reason for their parent's unhappiness could be a bad day at the office, for example. They've never had a bad day at the office and assume everything has something to do with them, especially when dysfunctional parents change their attitude to the children depending on their mood. Children are simply unable to meet the emotional needs of an adult.

Looking back I realise I was beginning to feel anxious at a very early age. I was always looking to figure out what mood my parents were in, and if they were not happy I felt pressure to make them feel better.

The narcissists do not like to take responsibility for their negative emotions, and transfer the blame to others. Further, they don't like to deal with any of the children's negative feelings. My mother's attitude was that children have no problems, and they should be a pleasure and a joy for their parent.

As a small child, it never occurred to me to question my parents and why they did not respond to any of my problems. If I was having bad feelings it was because something was wrong with me and I wasn't the joy I was supposed to be.

Back when I was a kid, my mother's narcissistic parenting was working well for her. I did not want to make her sick, or make her feel bad, and I was a very obedient kid. Making her feel good made me feel good, I loved helping in the house and getting praise for doing a good job. When she was happy with me everything was fine.

This is a common experience for many victims. Responsive, well-behaved small children bring the best out of the narcissistic parent, or at least the most caring side that looks after their physical needs. On top of this, small kids are cute and evoke maternal feelings; it is nature's way of protecting them during their vulnerable years.

The neediness and the worshiping are rewarding for the narcissists, and they thrive as parents of small children. My mother certainly did. Mind you, I was a very good toddler, trying very hard to please.

Unfortunately, this early attachment continues even after the narcissistic parent drastically changes their behaviour as the child grows up. The need to earn the approval of the parent gets well and truly entrenched in the brains of all children, but especially in those raised to be people pleasers.

FIRST TELLING MEMORIES

Even though many victims of narcissistic parents recall they knew something was wrong with their seemingly good parent when they were very young, as they grew up they still ended up blaming themselves for being fundamentally flawed and never good enough. That was true for me as well.

My first memories of sensing something was not right with my mother were around the age of five. I was going to preschool in the neighbourhood, and I was a rather shy and self-conscious kid.

A girl from my group happened to visit one evening with her grandfather. She was full of life; she was spinning, running around, and laughing a lot. Later, I heard my grandparents say, 'What a happy child,' in a way that made me believe that it was a good thing. The next day I started spinning happily around in the presence of my mother, much like the other girl had.

Her reaction was instant and unexpected. 'Stop, stop it now! Do you hear me, stop it! Stop it or I won't love you!' She had lost it completely, she was shaking, her face was tense with anger. She was so mad it was obvious even to a five-year-old that it was a reaction well out of proportion, and a vicious one at that.

'Why won't you love me because I am spinning around?' I wanted to ask, then thought better of it and stopped. Trying to be like that girl my grandparents liked made my mother mad. There was, however, another insightful and mature thought in my five-year-old head, which could be translated into the more grown-up observation: 'There is something very wrong with that woman.'

The other girl was full of energy and wasn't often worried or sad. I, on the other hand, was anxious and worried, and wanted to be liked and praised. In retrospect, the same girl was in the same school with me for many years, and she went through life with ease while I struggled.

Now I understand that what she had was unshakable love for herself, but not in the way the narcissists do. She did not look for validation from others, and did not have the anger and malice the narcissists have when they don't get what they think they deserve. Her self-love came from some source inside and she was happy with who she was and what she had.

The narcissistic disorder, on the other hand, demands others participate in the illusion. Their ego comes from the narcissistic shell and not from who they truly are.

Anyhow, the memory of my mother's extreme reaction was forgotten. Much, much later, in my early 40s, I remembered it and I understood what it was about.

It was not the action that provoked the narcissistic rage, but it was the unsolicited feeling, the spontaneous happiness and freedom I was expressing that was not acceptable to my mother. Suddenly she found I was out of control, doing and feeling something out of her reach. The truth is that the happier and stronger you are, the more unhappy the narcissistic parent is, because when you feel good they lose their grip over you, and the ability to shame you.

...

This was not the only time I knew something was very wrong.

An even earlier memory I can recall was my mother telling some woman an embarrassing toddler poop story involving me, and how glad she was that this part of motherhood was over. She was friendly and animated, and the other woman was agreeing.

I felt embarrassed and betrayed that she was talking about me as if I wasn't there, and after the woman left I asked her nicely not to tell embarrassing stories about me to others.

My mother's reaction was, 'Well, you won't let me say anything.' She was instantly annoyed and angry. All her friendliness was gone. This is ridiculous, I thought. It was my first time requesting this, and it was not unreasonable to ask not to be humiliated in front of others.

I am using this memory not because it was important or because it had some terrible impact on me, but because it was a very early indication of what was to become an increasingly damaging pattern of behaviour.

Getting angry when something about their behaviour is challenged in the nicest way, is a typical reaction of a narcissistic parent. My mother reacted as an angry child, but this was only the beginning of a consistent pattern of minimising my feelings with negative reactions, laughter, and humiliation.

Narcissists don't see their children as separate people that have a right to experience life from their own angle. There is no option in their heads in which the kids will be in charge of their own lives 'unaided' by the narcissist.

...

This is another relevant childhood memory:

At the seaside, my brother and my father went on the Ferris wheel; my brother got sick and threw up in his new hat. He was upset and embarrassed about it, but my mother would not let it go. That story was told and retold, and we were reminded of it every time we were near the seaside or a Ferris wheel. I could see my brother squirming every time, but she just carried on and on. It made me angry because she was tormenting him, and I was very sensitive to such things.

Much, much later, I figured out the real reason behind it. Not ever wanting to go on a Ferris wheel herself, my mother was against them going in the first place. She provided dire warnings, but my brother and father went anyway. My brother got sick and my mother was vindicated, and her being right was more important than the feelings of my brother. Come to think of it, she might have failed to notice his feelings completely – otherwise she might have figured out it was working against her image as a good mother.

My mother could not swim, which made summer holidays an exercise of smothering. We were not allowed to be in the water for more than two minutes. Around us, happy children splashed all day in the water and played in the sun. We had to stay under the shade of the small umbrella because she would not let us use sunscreen. As a good mother she didn't want to put 'anything dangerous' on our skin. When I pointed that she put cream on her face every single day, she got angry with me and made the familiar face with the chin up and lips tight and I got the familiar sinking reaction in my stomach.

Reasoning never works with narcissists. When caught in the game they get stroppy and angry. Their lack of emotional maturity and empathy is why the narcissistic parent cannot respond to the emotional needs of their children. They are too busy trying to get the validation they need, and that consumes a lot of their energy and effort.

The same happened when it was time for me to learn to drive. 'You? You cannot drive!' my mother told me, disgusted that I dared to bring that up. She could not drive and that meant I couldn't either. If I could, she would potentially lose some control down the line, and that was unacceptable.

It was an emotional statement and it had no reasoning behind it. Yet she was confident I was incapable of doing something the majority of people managed just fine. The needs of a narcissist always come first, and her need to feel she was superior to me was overriding any other considerations.

…

Of course, as a kid I did not analyse my mother's behaviour. Children adapt to the family dynamics the best they can. They might feel the atmosphere is unpleasant – I know I did – but they are not in a position to change it. All these things I knew as a small kid that bothered me – my mother's lack of empathy for my brother's pain, the strange reactions to my feelings – all those memories got pushed to the back of my mind, because I didn't know what to do about them.

…

Another example I recall was when a friend had chickenpox and her parents apparently offered my mother a play date so I could get it over and done with as well, because the illness is much safer and easier on small children.

She came straight to me, fuming with self-righteousness. 'What? I will never do that. I will not let my child get sick on purpose!' she was saying, pointing out what a good mother she was. 'I will never do that. What kind of parent will do that?' she was asking me as if I was supposed to know the answer.

Back then, I didn't know what to think. I knew the parents of my friend were just fine; they were good to me too. I didn't know what to think about infecting kids on purpose till I got chickenpox when I was twenty-five and alone in a new city. I had a fever and insomnia, itchy spots inside my ears and on the soles of my feet. It was nerve-wracking and painful and left a few marks. This is when I knew what to think about my mother's self-promotion as being the best mother around.

HOW DO THE NARCISSISTS GET AWAY WITH THE THINGS THEY DO FOR SO LONG?

Covert narcissists, as the name implies, are very good at hiding their true needy and abusive nature. And because the narcissistic mothers enjoy having small children, a presumption is created that they are good mothers. And they are not shy of actively promoting the image of the good mother – repeatedly telling you how much they sacrifice for you and brainwashing your perceptions of who they really are.

Another reason that the narcissists enjoy having small children is their energy and zest for life. I recall waking up in the morning and being instantly excited about the day ahead and everything about it. The narcissists like sucking that energy – they like kids when they are a delight, when they are full of life, when they are interesting and needy, filling their days and feeding their egos. The narcissistic expectation is that the child will serve that very purpose for life.

During this time, the narcissists appear to be normal parents taking care of the everyday needs of their children, like food and clothes. Underneath that, however, there are other things happening. The abuse is subtle, starts small and grows over time, and it's eroding that very same passion and energy for life.

CONDITIONAL LOVE

To have the children behave in a pleasing manner, the narcissistic mothers use conditional love and fear, sending the message the kids will be shunned and the love taken away it they step out of line.

When the parent is well and pleased the child is recognised. This is an easy and effective method of control, and all parents probably use it at one time or another, but most parents recognise their child's behaviour is not only about their own needs.

The narcissists use the conditional love method of parenting along with self-righteousness and open confidence that this is what a parent should do and that this is the best way to raise 'good children.' Narcissistic mothers do not have the maturity, empathy, or any desire to acknowledge their kids are their own persons who will one day have to go out into the world, because they want to control them indefinitely.

Controlling kids by making them responsible for the emotions, the well-being, and the decisions of the parents, is a sure way to create a high level of anxiety in them. Being responsible for something you have no control over is confusing and stressful. Over long periods of time it affects the adrenal system and can have a long-term effect on the health of the children.

There are some other abusive techniques that the narcissists employ very early on to control the behaviour of their offspring.

SILENT TREATMENT

As a punishment for misbehaving, my father used to smack me on the bottom. My mother's method of punishment was more effective than slapping. It was the silent treatment and the contempt she used to show towards me. I knew that disgusted look so well; her chin would go up, her lips pressed tight, her face screwed-up in contempt. It was such a sudden, drastic, and unpleasant change from the good mother when she was pleased, that my stomach would turn every time and I would wholeheartedly try to please her.

'You are not my child. No child of mine will do that,' was a statement my mother used often. Her proclaimed motherly love was gone in a heartbeat. I remember how scared it made me feel, a bit like my mother leaving and possibly never coming back again. It was a powerful survival fear. I was suddenly ostracised, and the feeling of shame and helplessness was overwhelming.

It never occurred to me as a child that this was a covert type of abuse. I only knew it made me feel undeserving of love and attention. Silent treatment cannot be argued with, it's based on emotions and not on logic. The line of communication is cut off, and it means the existence of the child can be reduced to nothing. Silent treatment is a power play, the parent is in the position to abandon the child, no explanations required. It does not offer solutions, and does not require effort on the part of the parent.

It worked very well though. I was fearful of upsetting my mother, as well as of upsetting any other adult. I already knew I was not liked for who I was because I was not good-looking and I was not clever like my brother. This is why I had to try harder to please, to justify my existence and earn love. This was the image of myself mirrored to me, and the expectations placed on me. And when I failed, there was nothing I could fall back on. Such early childhood conditioning is what creates toxic shame and people pleasers.

The silent treatment is a tool of parents who are immature and angry and do not have the understanding that they are the adults and that they have to help the children deal with negative things. Instead they pile their own issues and negativity on top, under the assumption they will shame and scare their children into behaving the way they want them to. Unfortunately, it is very damaging to the development of the children, and it does not work in the long run.

Please don't get me wrong – every parent might shame their kids once in a while. Shame is necessary when it's in the right context. Non-narcissistic parents yell on occasion, get fed up and smack their offspring. As long as they have good communication in general and the parents apologise and talk about it, it would just be a part of life. Life is messy; it's not black or white.

What I am talking about here is the systematic use of the punishment to demean and to avoid explanations the narcissists are not comfortable with. The control is achieved by the means of humiliating and terrifying a child.

TOXIC SHAME

Parents have major influence over their children; they are the providers of care and security. They are models for the behaviour of the children, for understanding how the world works, who they are, and how they see themselves. The parents are a mirror the children see themselves in, and the influence continues as they grow.

The narcissists mirror only what is good for them. They don't have the capacity to see the child as a separate entity, or to empathise and respond to what the child feels or with what the child needs to hear.

Unfortunately, the way the narcissistic mothers establish control is through instilling guilt, duty, and shame. They are powerful manipulation tools. Once such feelings become a prevalent reason for the behaviour of the child, they turn into something that is called toxic shame, and toxic shame is so destructive it stops the child from becoming a healthy and functioning adult.

Toxic shame is believing you are inherently wrong, inadequate, insufficient. Believing that if people see who you truly are they will be disgusted as much as you are. It leads to catastrophising and self-hatred as a way of life, to anxiety and mental paralysis. It leads to a harsh inner voice and inability to relax and enjoy life.

Ironically, toxic shame is in the centre of the narcissistic disorder as well, but the narcissistic shell is there to never let it out. The false image is that they are the greatest, and they are not. Their children end up thinking they are the worst, but they are not. Both conditions can lead to personality disorders.

In both cases the toxic shame is dealt with differently, but it's the same thing: refusal to accept who you are and all human aspects of your nature. Toxic shame is a result of long-term abuse by someone in a position of power twisting the victim's perception of reality. I experienced the same reaction to rejection for decades, the same shameful sinking and paralysing feeling of helplessness and humiliation.

Examples of silent treatment:

Once I got the silent treatment for taking coins from the pockets of the coats hanging at the door. It was clear to me what I did was wrong even though I was four or five.

Other times, however, it was not so clear.

I had a little bag that I treasured. A story often told and retold by my mother was that I had said something cute to my mother's boss and he was so impressed he gave the bag to me.

The second time I met my mother's boss, I knew I was expected to repeat my triumph and say something clever and cute again. I froze and could not think of anything to say. Afterwards, my mother had the tight-lipped face and did not talk to me for quite some time.

That made me confused and angry. I just wasn't clever enough and didn't know what to do about it. The bag was tainted, and the story of me being clever was tainted as well.

That time, the silent treatment was confusing. I was punished for not saying something to entertain and impress, and my failure felt bitter and unresolved.

But there was something else that was even more confusing.

CRAZY MAKING

One morning, my mother was very upset at me. Apparently I did something in her dream, something shameful she implied, but she would not say what. Of course I got upset because she was upset and because I was apparently the reason for it. The accusation came clearly out of nowhere. I felt she was disturbed, or disgusted, and there was some animosity in the mix, and I was shaken by that sudden emotional attack.

After a while she appeared to let it go. 'No, you wouldn't do that, would you? You are a good girl,' she finally declared, and carried on.

She had let my disgusting behaviour go because she was such a good forgiving mother despite the fact I did bad things in her dream. And I was left standing there, feeling upset at the unfounded accusations, and dirty for some reason I could not understand.

This is called crazy making, and it is what narcissists do. They push to provoke bad feelings, and when they do and their victim reacts, they feel better. Somehow they transfer their state of mind onto their victims. It is hard for a normal person to comprehend how and why that works, but reason is not what narcissists work with. Somehow they are justified because someone else gets the bad feelings and they have 'cleared' themselves.

MANIPULATION

Though they are the absolute power when it comes to their children, the covert narcissists are not strong, able, or secure people, and this is why they use manipulation as a way of life.

An example:

As the good mother she considered herself to be, my mother was proud of the fact that we ate home-cooked meals, and encouraged us to eat. Food was important to her image as a mother. On the weekend, however, when my father took the family hiking, we each got only one small sandwich and I got mocked if I ate it too early.

I knew my father was against eating too much in general, he was constantly trying to lose weight and failing to do so. Yet I could not understand why my mother's entire attitude towards food and eating was suddenly different. I could not understand why she was making fun of me for something I was normally encouraged to do.

Now I have a better idea of what was going on.

Covert narcissists change their attitude depending on who they want to project their image to. My father was at work all day and my mother was showing us what a good mother she was with food, but she easily changed her behaviour to target my father, not caring at all about the inconsistency in her behaviour.

This example is a small thing, but over time those inconsistencies become more and more and create a sense of betrayal and confusion.

The narcissists strive to project a sweet and caring image of a highly moral person. From such a high stand they can judge those around them for their failings and demand they behave in a manner that serves the narcissists better.

Throughout my life, my 'good' mother used to put me down in front of her friends, to talk against my father and brother to me, against my grandparents to all, against me to my father, and against her friends in front of me, and each time she presented herself as the victim. Somehow none of this appeared unethical to her.

Talking others into submission is a major narcissistic skill. Twisting things their way is how they keep their false image. If you listen only to their words they sound convincing, but if you look at what they are doing and the relationships they have, it is a different story.

TRIANGULATION

Talking about someone to another person instead of communicating directly is called triangulation, and it is about controlling the flow of information. It is a manipulation technique that works only in families with broken dysfunctional communication, and it is a perfect tool for a narcissist. They can create tension between the members of the family and benefit from it by playing the one who solves all problems. It is another way of getting in a higher position of influence.

I was an adult when I finally figured what my mother had been doing all along.

There are other techniques narcissists use, I will list some below. If you are an adult child of a covert narcissist you were in the worst position possible, because you never had a normal upbringing to compare their behaviour to.

Once I began to understand what was done to me I got very angry and upset. If you feel the same way reading this book, please realise that you never knew what normal was and you were not in a position to change your situation as a child. The fact that you survived without turning into a narcissist means you were stronger. Be kind to yourself.

MINIMISING, DEMEANING

As I mentioned above, according to my mother's views that 'children should be a joy' and 'children have no problems,' I wasn't allowed to complain or have negative feelings. I did have them, of course. Children experience their 'small' problems as much as anybody, they are proportional to their life experience. All children need reassurance, and help to deal with their negative feelings. Instead of helping, narcissistic mothers make the problems worse.

An example:

I had a problem, and it was the way I looked. I was not what was beautiful, that was made clear to me by my mother. 'We were hoping you would have thick hair like your father and my eyes, but, well, it's not what happened …,' she explained the situation to me, without even trying to find something good to say to soften the blow.

I remember being very frustrated with that, because there was nothing I could do about it. I was looking for some way to feel good about my looks, at least a little bit. And I wanted to be liked, to be like those princesses from the fairy tales. Knowing I didn't look good made me feel angry and unpleasant inside, and ashamed I was not up to expectations.

I tried to recall a single compliment related to me and not to my pleasing behaviour during my childhood, but I could not. Both my parents liked to point out only the negative things. My father was not a narcissist, but he was a narcissistic enabler and a socially inadequate man who was abusive in a traditional way. Not surprisingly, all abusers use mockery and humiliation to minimise their victims.

WHY NARCISSISTS NEED ENABLERS

The covert narcissists are vulnerable to worry; they do not have the blunt self-confidence of the overt narcissists. They suffer stress and anxiety, and use much of their energy to maintain the illusion they are such exceptional people.

In addition, the covert narcissists are static, they do nothing to change themselves or their circumstances, because they believe they are complete as they are and that others should know they are special without having to prove anything. The false image demands that others must look after the narcissists, follow their lead and fulfil their desires. The shell protects the false image by projecting blame to others if things don't go their way. People with the disorder do not perceive reality the way most people do.

Because the covert narcissists are not very good achievers, and because of their need for supply, they need a spouse who is easy to manipulate and who will not call them out on their bullshit – someone to deal with real life while the narcissists are busy maintaining the illusion of how great they are.

NARCISSISTIC ENABLERS

The spouses of narcissists cannot be independent or emotionally secure people. They are there to maintain the atmosphere the narcissists can thrive in, and this is the toxic atmosphere of miscommunication and tension that allows them to play their games and to be the 'good one.'

Normal people don't engage with narcissists for long, because they figure that something is not quite right with them and move on rather quickly. And the opposite is true: the narcissists do not thrive in the presence of normal people. Hence their choice of friends and spouses is of people who will not challenge their behaviour.

My father was a good provider, and he was a workaholic and a perfectionist. He didn't know how to communicate with us, disliked socialising, and had a lot of bottled anger against the world. He was always upset about someone or something, about the wrong people being in power or getting recognition instead of him. He was a traditional man, with very traditional and rigid values, and was abusive in a traditional way. Unlike my mother, his faults were obvious even to a child.

On occasion, he took his anger out on us. His main target was my brother, probably because he was more rebellious and smart and that rubbed my father the wrong way. He attacked my brother for 'talking too much,' or 'philosophising'—used as a demeaning term.

My brother was four years older and a very clever boy. He could play chess as a kid and was exceptionally good at maths and physics, managed to build a radio from parts when he was twelve, and ended up getting a degree in astrophysics.

As a small child, my father used to tease him to tears, and he appeared quite satisfied when he made him cry. My brother was a sensitive child as well, but he was more defiant than me, probably because he was openly harassed by my father.

I saw my father physically assault my brother only once, but it was very ugly and upsetting. I felt so bad for him I told my mother and asked her to do something. At first she didn't believe me, but I was insistent. The next day, she said she had spoken to my father and he wasn't going to do it again. She had the self-satisfied expression of 'see, I resolved everything.'

It was a typical reaction of a narcissistic mother. There was no more talking about the incident, no explanations, no apologies, no acknowledgement of what had happened. Just uncomfortable silence. Yet she claimed the glory without solving anything.

After that, the atmosphere in the house was more uncomfortable and noxious than ever. For the next several years my father and brother avoided each other, and my mother unloaded her frustrations with both of them onto me.

The point I am trying to make is that all abusers do the same thing – they diminish and minimise their children to make themselves bigger and better, or because they are scared or angry or inadequate – but the narcissists, and especially the covert narcissists, hide their abuse and their victims do not even realise they are being slowly undermined and destroyed.

They are so much harder to fight, and their abuse is with you even when you are an adult, mostly because the narcissistic parent is still there, while the open abuser is easier to get rid of.

My mother did her diminishing and minimising under the cover of care. I think my much smarter brother figured it out earlier, but I remained in her games till I was an adult. My sensitive nature did not help the matter, because I became a hopeless people pleaser and an emotional sponge. The guilt and shame my mother was dishing freely went into each fibre of my being.

To do that successfully she needed the dysfunctional environment my father was a big part of, because she had a lot more room in which to manipulate. And there was no one to call her out on her dysfunction, because he could never figure out my mother's complex manipulations.

They had very different expectations of what we should be like. My father wanted us to go out and do things, because he was socially inept himself, and my mother was doing her best to keep us naïve, scared, and dependent, because in her plans her high position in life was that of a mother who rules her children and grandchildren under her roof.

And this is why narcissists damage their children and create invisible wounds that would make them susceptible to manipulation. The narcissistic parent needs to be perceived as better and more capable – it gives them a sense of control and is probably the only way that is acceptable to their false image.

DYSFUNCTIONAL FAMILIES

A prevalent atmosphere of negativity is a sure sign of dysfunctional parents. My mother liked pointing out our shortcomings, and so did my father. I don't think he was capable of understanding how badly that was affecting us, but my mother had a whole consistent strategy in place to ensure getting supply for life.

Dysfunctional families are made by parents with personality disorders, or psychological problems, or just people who have unrealistic expectations and have demands the children cannot meet. If a parent does not know how to deal with money, for example, they will not be able to teach their children how to be good with money. And if the parents do not know how to handle emotional problems in a healthy way, they will not teach their children how to do that.

Nobody likes to talk about mentally unfit parents and the damage they do to their children, because it's a difficult problem to resolve. Yet the only way to deal with abuse and dysfunction is to bring the issues out into the light and talk about them.

Growing up in an atmosphere of constant negativity and criticism is not obvious abuse, yet it does great damage. There was a time my father decided to teach me how to ski. The pressure on me to perform was so great I choked more often than not, and then my father would make disappointed grunts and noises. I was both scared and humiliated to disappoint him, and quite unhappy about the whole thing. It was not a weekend out; it was torture I could not wait to be over.

My father could not comprehend that one cannot create resilient kids by abusing them, but by helping them cope well when they fail. He could not cope well, and he took his frustration out on us. Needless to say, we did not end up more resilient. It's a cycle of abuse not easily broken.

From the point of view of a forty-year-old, I can sympathise with the child I was – eager to please and trying so hard – but when I was seven I thought I was useless and that it was my fault I was such a disappointment.

As a small kid, I thought my mother was the good parent and it took me years and years to realise the opposite was true.

Despite his faults and problems, my father was more functional and less destructive as a parent. He taught me to drive, for example, even if as though it was his 'duty' and not desire. He had the human ability to empathise and love, though he had no idea how to show it and he followed my mother's lead.

HOW NARCISSISTS UNDERMINE AND ERODE YOUR PERSONALITY

One way of undermining their children's confidence and showing their superiority as parents, is by laughing at them.

This is abuse they can disguise and get away with so easily, and it can do more damage in the long run than physical violence. We are not talking about good-natured laughter, but nasty digs concealed as just a bit of fun.

People who have never experienced anything like it might say that this is not abuse, but it truly is. When you are left miserable and humiliated in an orchestrated and consistent manner, it is abuse and a major betrayal on the part of the parent.

An example:

My father used to cut my hair very short, a standard boy's haircut. I was told my hair was too thin, and that keeping it very short would make it thicker, but I think it had a lot to do with his obsessive-compulsive personality traits.

I hated the haircut and the whole humiliating process, but I was an obedient child and not doing what they told me to do was unthinkable. I did not run away or protest much, but holding my tears back proved impossible each time. It had become a sort of family event, with both of them hovering around me and waiting for me to start crying and to justify their expectations.

I was sitting patiently, hair falling around my eyes, and at the end the result was always the same – I looked ugly and not at all like the girl I wanted to look like and I could not stop the tears dropping down my cheeks.

'There she goes crying again ...' Both were triumphant for some reason and that made me cry even more. I felt betrayed, weak, helpless, hurt, and angry with myself. The main reason for it was my parents' perplexing attitude; as if they were waiting for a confirmation of what they already knew and had pointed out to me – that I was unattractive and weak. There was no empathy for my tears, no desire to make any attempt to make me feel better.

TOXIC SHAME RESPONSE

Looking back, I understand why my response was to freeze. According to a number of academic sources there are three responses to abuse: fight, flight, and freeze. Shamed children respond with a freeze reaction. Shame is disempowering and paralyses the victim. It feels like you want to disappear, to become invisible so they will leave you alone. It is the response to being reduced and humiliated, and it has a lot to do with the feeling of helplessness – being caught up in a situation you cannot change.

People with a strong sense of self can take a joke. Good parents allow a child to develop that strong sense of self. Toxic parents do not. Even as an adult, that feeling of shame could bring me right back to that childhood state of misery. It's a shame of who you are, and it's not logical or rational at all. It is the result of a prolonged mental torment.

And if my father doing that was not a surprise, my 'good' mother mocking me was very confusing. She would act sympathetically when I scraped my knee or hurt myself physically in some way. The only conclusion was that I did not deserve sympathy for having bad emotions.

And there was the thing – not doing bad things was easier than not feeling bad emotions. They were piling up inside and suffocating me and the only way out was tears.

NARCISSISTIC ATTITUDE TO SMALL CHILDREN

Children are targeted by many types of abusers because they are soft targets – they are non-threatening and respond to the authority of adults.

My mother, for example, loved small children. 'Kids are so interesting at this age …,' she used to say about toddlers who had just learned to speak and to react to adult interaction.

Her interest stopped gradually as I was growing up, till at sixteen I found myself alone before surgery, getting anaesthetic and kind words from the surgical nurse. I was no longer a small child, the illusion of concern and care had worn off, and my mother had given up trying to show what a good mother she was.

Small children are the best source of supply, of unquestionable love and admiration. What small kids put on the table is blind loyalty and idealisation, acknowledgement the parents are the authority on all things, and listening and doing what they are told. If you are prepared to give the narcissists their drug they will be on their best behaviour towards you.

When I was a child, my mother could be generous at times with little treats like ice cream and chocolate bars. Covert narcissists appear quite normal and caring at times. That creates a good amount of confusion about who they really are. This is because the very young brain cannot process the complex dynamics of give and take in a mature way. The generosity was because I was still a child worshiping her and she was getting her supply and living in her world of narcissistic expectations.

As the children grow up and try to be their own people, the narcissistic parents lose interest. Bad sources of supply are devalued with a great deal of rage, and the attitude towards the offspring changes drastically.

As I became a teenager, any request – no matter how reasonable – was faced with frustration. Growing up and trying to have your own values and personality is not received well, and the narcissistic parent will try to sabotage you any way they can.

SUMMARY OF EARLY CHILDHOOD MEMORIES

If any of the above sounded familiar it is likely you are a child of a covert narcissist. And, if so, you probably have some good memories from this time. The early childhood memories have a very powerful influence, and this is why the shame and guilt still work on adult children of narcissists.

You have to understand the dynamics behind the narcissistic façade and why you ended up broken and down, in order to reverse the damage.

As an adult, you must learn to embrace your human side and to combat the toxic shame. Remember, everyone is human. What's been instilled in you is a lot of dysfunction. Awareness is the enemy of all narcissists.

THE EARLY FOUNDATIONS OF BAD MENTAL HEALTH AND SELF-DESTRUCTION

My mother's covert narcissistic behaviour was creating destructive negativity and self-hatred because it targeted the most inner and important part – who I was and what I thought of myself.

This is where toxic shame and anxiety begin. The message I got was that I was faulty and flawed by nature, and I had to perform to be accepted, and earn love by pleasing.

Children of narcissists get confusing ideas about what love is. The love is conditional on the child's ability to hide their true, 'inconvenient' needs and emotions. The message is that they are not worthy and only valued if they justify their existence by pleasing those around them.

The catch, of course, is that they will never please enough. The narcissist will never get enough validation, because it's a personality disorder that escalates with time and with circumstances.

If you are an adult child of a narcissist, it's likely that you feel bad about feeling good, as if you are not entitled to feel good or to being told good things. It's because you are not comfortable in your own skin.

Ironically, what the narcissistic parents destroyed in you is the healthy narcissism children require to grow up as healthy adults.

PART II: Covert Narcissistic Mothers and Children

The classic narcissistic approach is to pick the child that is most likely to mirror the parent and provide supply, and make him or her the Golden Child. The child that senses something is wrong and challenges the narcissist becomes the Scapegoat. In between, are the Lost Child – the one that knows something is wrong, but still strives to please and keep the peace – and the Mascot, who tries to take the pressure off by entertaining the others.

My brother was my mother's favourite; he had both good looks and exceptional abilities in maths and physics. My mother was trying to make a connection with him like she never tried with me. I think my brother was my mother's Golden Child, but he was my father's target for abuse and became rebellious early on.

I was the Lost Child at the start, but somehow we both ended up as Scapegoats. Both of us could see and feel the dysfunction in the family, but he figured out or reacted to it much earlier than I did.

When he stopped providing supply for my mother she was endlessly complaining to me, saying he was 'acting up' and had 'such difficult character.' It was her way of attaching the problem to him and keeping herself clear of any responsibility or blame.

Of course, when she was complaining about my father he was the one with the difficult character, and later, when I stopped listening to her complaints, she accused me of having difficult character.

My brother's story is not mine to tell and I will stick with mine from this point on.

As a child, I fitted in the category of the Lost Child: quiet, trying to please everyone and to keep the peace in the family. I was reading a lot and I wasn't complaining or wanting to bring attention to myself. I was the one who listened to my mother's endless complaints, and felt bad for my brother, and had to endure weekend trips with my father.

And while I was not getting in trouble with my parents much, I was not getting my emotional needs met at all. Instead I was keeping everything inside and trying to be whatever they wanted me to be.

THE LOST CHILD

When I started school, everything was going seemingly well for my mother. I was a very good girl, one of the best students. I wanted to please my teachers and when I failed I had an unpleasant sinking feeling in my stomach. When I messed up my assignments I wanted to cry, and sometimes I did. My mother found that funny and she would laugh about it without making any effort to understand the reason for my anxiety or to help me feel better.

Trying hard and being conscientious was considered good behaviour for a child, but mixed with toxic shame it had certain crippling effects on me.

Some examples:

In the first year of school I made three rag dolls, my teacher took them to show other teachers and I never got them back. 'Where are your dolls?' My mother asked me, and I said I didn't know.

I knew they were in a cupboard in the classroom, I had seen them there. I couldn't ask to have them back because my teacher had told everybody how good I was, and I could never bring myself to disappoint her by demanding she give them back to me.

There was another impossible task: telling my mother that I couldn't bring myself to ask the teacher to give me back the dolls. I could not bring myself to ever bring up the subject again. Both could damage the good impression I had made and lessen the high prize I had received.

Back then, I could vaguely sense that it was a problem. I did not know what people pleasing was, but I knew something was not quite right with me. Being so shy was not good, I knew that at some level, but did not have a clue how to change that.

At this stage I still adored my mother with the blind devotion of a child and thought she was the good parent in the family. My grandparents gave me money for Christmas and I immediately spent it on presents for my mother – flowers, table cloths, necklaces, and all sorts of silly things. It made her happy and pleased, and that gave me a nice secure feeling inside.

At the same time, I found it strange that she wasn't telling me to stop spending money. In our very frugal family everyone got one present, and spending money on silly things was very much frowned upon. Yet my mother gladly took to being the exception to the rule because her special status as a mother was validated, and nothing else superseded that.

This is a small example of the ability of the narcissists to see themselves differently than anyone else. They can take your love, loyalty, time, and effort to please gladly, because they think it's the way it should be, but they don't give any validation back. If you need them, their effort, their loyalty, you become a burden and you get frustration and blame instead.

The narcissists cannot help who they are, not even when they are trying to be good parents. My mother talked a lot about her day or whatever was on her mind, but listening and empathising with my problems was hard for her. That was the case even when she was obviously trying.

An example:

My mother was sharing her upset for the day: a work event on Saturday was very much ruffling feathers with everyone at the office because people liked their weekends free. My mother agreed with her colleagues, but somehow she was the one her boss was upset with. 'How was I to know he came up with the idea?' she was saying. 'He looked at me, as if it was all my doing … They put me in such a bad situation …' and so on.

She spoke with conviction, I could hear the upset in her voice, and I got upset as well. My heart was beating faster and I felt her pain and the associated feelings of being in an awkward situation. My mother was talking away – she was innocent, others were to blame and she had strong empathy for herself.

I had a similar problem and I decided to share it, something I would not normally do. This was my problem at the age of ten:

We were a group of four friends coming back from school together because we lived in the same neighbourhood and because we got along and had fun. There was a new 'thing' – a winter scarf, one baggy, stretchy, long piece of fabric you could wrap around in many ways. We were going to go together to the place they were sold. I didn't like the scarf and said it was stupid, and one of the girls took offence. They went without me and told me what a jolly good time they had, and that I was stupid for not liking the scarf.

I felt hurt and left out because they shut me out of the group. I was a sensitive girl trying to avoid confrontations of any kind. Being left out came out of nowhere, and I had a shameful, guilty feeling that I had made a huge mistake and would not be accepted as their friend again.

My mother made an effort to figure out what to say, she had the tense expression of someone thinking hard, then she brightly suggested I go to the scarf sale alone.

I said I was hurt because I was left behind, not because I wanted a scarf. I knew at some level that the other girls were overreacting. All I said was I didn't like the scarf, and I didn't call anyone stupid. What I really needed to hear was that I should not worry about that too much, and that I shouldn't feel so bad.

My mother put her thinking face on again, but she got annoyed very quickly. 'Well, next time don't say anything.' That was the best she could do, and then lost interest in my problem. On top of that she looked annoyed with me.

Her comment made my pain worse because I already blamed myself for causing the situation and she confirmed it was my fault.

As a child I was searching for her to acknowledge my value as a person. My mother wouldn't, or she couldn't. Somehow she managed to make things worse by targeting the insecurities I had.

Back then, I wondered how she could have so much empathy for herself but not for me. As if it was not possible for her to get out of her head and understand that my problems were valid, or even existing.

This is a major issue with all narcissistic parents, and it was with my mother. Everything she could relate to had to do with her. What I said or did was automatically in connection with her needs or wants, with the protection of her false image. Her idea of being an exceptional mother was just that, an image she had of herself, and she could not even see me as a person.

LACK OF EMPATHY

This lack of empathy is one of the main characteristics of the disorder. For whatever reason, the development of the narcissists was stunted and they did not master the ability to empathise. They appear to be unable to get out of their heads and their reality and understand what another human being might be feeling.

This might not be so bad by itself, but the emotional development of their children depends on them. Parents have such authoritarian power it is impossible for the children not to get affected by their disorder.

At best, narcissists try, but they cannot handle anybody's problems like mature adults because of the urgent and all-consuming need to keep the false image, their egos, and their false, unrealistic state of supremacy going.

Eventually, as all children of narcissists, I stopped talking about my problems, and a big part of my childhood communication with my mother was listening to her talk and getting upset about her problems. Yet I was afraid to share my problems out of fear my mother was going to make them worse.

This chronic lack of empathy distorts the borders in the parent-child relationship.

DISTORTED BORDERS

Having good borders is very important for good mental health. Children of narcissists do not get to develop good borders. Being responsible for the emotions and the wellbeing of the parent has severe consequences on the developing brain, because the lack of control and coping skills creates chronic tension and anxiety.

The children are always on the lookout for the moods of their parent, but making the adults happy is a very tall order. The danger of displeased parents and the instability it brings are always present, and the brain responds to danger because evolutionarily it's critical to survival.

Borders are there to separate the self from the others. In a narcissistic family, the borders are distorted by the demands of the disorder, and the responsibility for the mental state of the parent is put on the children who are not allowed to express their true feelings.

This is how co-dependency develops early in life to support the narcissistic parent. It appears the children of the narcissists somehow balance the lack of empathy the narcissists have by becoming very sensitive empaths, and feeling other people's feelings while having a very fractured sense of self, of belonging, and of personal value.

I can clearly recall feeling very bad for my classmates who could not answer the questions of the teacher. As a school child I wanted to please not only my teachers, but was also the peacemaker between friends and didn't want to see anyone upset. My shame-based upbringing was about making others feel good, not only my parents. It was a way of placing myself in the world.

Later in life, at the peak of my disorder, the anxiety had progressed so much I was not able to watch TV shows because I felt so bad for the characters if there was any drama or danger involved. I was overwhelmed by their emotions to such a degree that my muscles would constrict and my breathing would change. The exact same thing happened when I had to interact with people, and I was unable to turn it off.

EARLY SIGNS OF ANXIETY

An example:

As a child, my self-esteem was very much about performance. Failing to perform was my biggest fear, and it's fair to say it was an emotional reaction, and not a logical one.

When I got a C in maths my stomach was in knots for two days before I told my mother. She gasped, ready to tear into me, but she decided to change to the 'good mother' and said in an authoritarian, motherly way, 'You will get a better mark next time, won't you,' and I was so grateful and relieved.

Looking back, one bad mark that had happened mostly due to bad circumstances, involved a disproportional amount of agony for me.

The fear of failure was making every day at school stressful. I didn't know what anxiety was, or why my stomach was convulsing before maths classes. I wasn't good at maths, and if I failed to perform I knew I'd somehow end up being less then I was before.

It was the toxic shame that comes with having a narcissistic parent. Whether it is intentional, or just a side effect of their own disorder, narcissists strip their children of worth. Only the parent matters, it is the default and over time this dysfunctional relationship does very serious and lasting damage.

PEOPLE PLEASING AND TOXIC SHAME

As I mentioned before, the base of toxic shame is the belief one is flawed and unworthy, and – as such – undeserving to feel or have good things in their lives. Physical reactions to toxic shame include heat around the forehead and nasal passages, muscle tension and a clenched jaw, and heaviness in the chest and stomach. In the long term, it can affect posture and breathing patterns.

Children who are accepted and loved only when responding to the needs and desires of their parents, become people pleasers who see their value in relation to the satisfaction of others with them. The punishment for failing to please is rejection and abandonment, and it is the worst thing for a child.

To me, it seemed very important to keep on getting good grades and praise, because without that I had nothing to offer in return for acceptance and love. I felt there was danger in failing, because it felt like falling into some dark, bottomless pit. This is exactly what happened to me later, but as a child I could still keep up functioning somehow.

HOW THE COVERT NARCISSIST MAKES YOU FEEL FLAWED AND UNWORTHY

Covert narcissists make you feel flawed and unworthy by covert attacks on your appearance and on your character.

Some examples:

In a moment of good vibes between us, I asked my mother if I was good-looking. She paused, with her thinking face on, and said, 'Well, you are ... charming'. Yet as she was saying it she was letting me know something else was true. Her metalanguage – the wry face, the pause, the hand gesture – was that of dishonesty and displeasure. Of course I assumed the exact opposite was the truth, but she was such a good mother she had to lie to me.

Looking back with the eyes of an adult I understand I was a normal looking child, certainly not one that was evoking negative reaction in others. It was my mother's take on reality, and unfortunately she distorted my perception and I thought everyone was thinking I was ugly when they were looking at me.

Another example was her reaction when I got a compliment on my looks. A neighbour saw me in my school gymnastic outfit and exclaimed, 'Oh, how pretty you look.'

My mother recoiled at that, lips pressed tight, disbelief on her face. I could not tell whether she could not control her expressions or whether she was doing it on purpose, but the result was the same – a clear message to me I was below expectations. In the end I assumed the nice woman next door was a bit silly.

I was in the gymnastics team for a bit, but I felt I stood out. Some of those girls knew well they were pretty, and they knew how to giggle and have fun. In the end I tried to be the reliable one that gets the good marks at school. Yet the more self-conscious I felt and the harder I tried, the more mistakes I made and the more I failed.

Examples of covert attacks on the character:

In line with her 'children should bring joy' policy, my mother got annoyed when I got sick, because I was 'such a weakling.' Having the flu once a year wasn't being a weakling, I knew that, but she said it every time. She got sick every year as well, and that involved a lot of drama.

I recall having a bad cough and my mother getting very angry. 'Stop it, just stop it! What on earth is that?' She wasn't joking; the rage underneath came out. She was angry I wasn't fulfilling my unspoken contract. Narcissists expect you to be fit and healthy because the very reason for having children was so that they would be their supporters and allies, they are supposed to look after them and not to be a problem and a burden.

And, yes, to a degree every parent wishes for that, but most understand sickness is an unavoidable part of childhood and life, and have the emotional maturity and empathy not to attack their children when they are ill.

Unfortunately, when I had the flu my eyes watered excessively with every twinge in my blocked nose. What made this a truly miserable time was my parents' ritual of using that to humiliate me every time I was sick.

At the worst stage of the flu, both came to 'check how the weakling is doing' and stare at me, expecting to get the predictable reaction:

being stared at would make me self-conscious, the twinges in the nose would get worse, and tears would start dropping down my cheeks. This was what they were waiting for. 'There she goes ...,' my mother rejoiced, and both left the room satisfied they got what they came for.

I was ashamed and humiliated because I was so weak and predictable. Having the flu was equal to a failure of character. They had managed to reduce me to tears just by looking at me. I was a disappointment, unlikable, pitiful and undeserving.

This was my logic as a child, beating myself up for failing to live up to expectations. After they left I cried for real, a delayed reaction to the humiliation, and next time my reaction was even more instant and deplorable.

When I think back I wonder why I did not react in a more violent way to this torture, hide my face, or yell at them to stop it. No, I just stood there mortified and humiliated every time, year after year. It was the 'freeze' reaction of toxic shame, or maybe it was because of abuse while I was too young to retain any memories.

And instead of thinking, 'what kind of people would do this again and again,' I was angry and disappointed with myself. I had no knowledge of how to defend myself from humiliation and I was exactly the type of person the narcissists can feed on, because they can easily trigger the emotions they want.

When I felt I was about to get sick I experienced a range of anxieties. I was worried I'd miss out on school, get low grades, that I was about to get watery eyes and get humiliated, and those things were a lot worse than the illness itself.

WHY NARCISSISTIC PARENTS ABUSE

As a child, I could not understand why my parents behaved the way they did, but looking back as an adult I understand why this was happening.

My father's normal reaction to me being sick was a mild irritation and 'she will be fine.' He would certainly avoid awkwardness as much as I would. Those visits during the most vulnerable and unpleasant part of my illness were orchestrated by my mother, and the reason was very much her hidden narcissistic agenda.

My father's attitude towards the future of his children was the opposite of my mother's. He wanted us to do dangerous things, to go to places and be very successful. He wanted to send us out into the world as soon as possible.

My narcissistic mother's plan was to have us in her house and under her rule for life. She was rather small-minded, overly worried, and not very successful. Yet she believed she was something special even if she had nothing to show for it.

Motherhood is something a covert narcissist can successfully hide behind, because it comes with all the inbuilt power and preconceptions a narcissist can exploit. It can be a good excuse as well, the good old 'everything I did was for you.' We were her minions, her justification that she was the wisest and the most capable. She could not let us go out into the world.

She needed my father on her side as a provider to help her keep that control she craved so badly. This is where the narcissistic manipulation came into play. That's what the narcissists are very good at, because it is how they sustain their false image.

My mother used anything she could to show him that I was a sickling and a weakling. She wanted him to get used to the idea that I would need looking after and parental control for life.

Only my mother's sick mind could come up with that. It is hard to accept a mother can do that, but a covert narcissistic mother can. She managed to exaggerate my weaknesses and sabotage my strengths. It is sick, but that is why the narcissism is a disorder.

Covert narcissists are slow poison. It's a death by a thousand cuts, and their victims do not even realise they are being destroyed. She managed to bring me down so badly I ended up loathing myself and became suicidal later in life.

WAYS OF CONTROL

Covert narcissists are deeply dysfunctional, but very manipulative. Somehow, to cover up for their flaws, they must transfer what they don't like about themselves onto you. Believe it or not, this is a technique that is common; all humans like to blame others when things go wrong. But with narcissists it is a way of being. They never take responsibility or acknowledge their shortcomings.

My mother could control me just by looking at me in a particular way. She was very good at triggering the toxic shame in me. Although I was no longer confiding in her, I still had the need to be accepted. Ironically, I was striving for outside approval as much as my mother was, but my false image was the very opposite of hers and a lot more self-destructive in the short run.

As a result, I was not able to handle the disapproval of any authority figure. Any criticism or disapproval from an adult was evoking a hot, unpleasant sinking feeling.

I was sensing that I was paying a very high price for the approval I craved, but didn't have a clue why that was or what to do about it.

Shame and guilt are the weapons of the covert narcissists. The parents want children that do well, but stay firmly under their control and that are never seen as better than the narcissists. That creates very confused children, and not very successful ones, because they are paralysed with guilt and insecurity and do not know how to fight back. It becomes a self-fulfilling prophecy – the children are attacked for perceived faults so many times that they end up broken in the end.

DYNAMICS IN ABUSIVE FAMILIES

Toxic parents in general have some form of mental disorder, or at least strong tendencies of one. Such people have children expecting them to somehow fix whatever is wrong with their lives. That is not a realistic expectation, and when the children fail to do so the parents become angry and resentful. The children are clueless; they feel the resentment and take everything that is mirrored back to them to be true. The shortcomings, the frustrations, and the anger of the parents are passed on to the children.

An example:

My father was a perfectionist with compulsive tendencies. He decided to build a big house in my grandfather's yard, and it turned into an obsession dragging on for years. One day he was in a rotten mood and rounded up my brother and me to help him mix cement. I was sprinkling water with a hose while my brother was supposed to mix gravel and cement powder with a shovel longer then he was.

My brother was twelve, a skinny boy in shorts and a T-shirt. My father was grumpy and kept on yelling at him, he was struggling and finally refused to co-operate. My father lost the plot, he started swearing and kicking his small behind with such rage I simply froze.

He kept on kicking him, my brother was trying to get away but his way was blocked by building materials. My father kept on chasing after him and kicking him so hard every time that his small body was propelled forward and he nearly lost his balance, till finally he managed to run down the street. My father came back, swearing away, his face twisted, out of control rage spilling out of him.

I just stood there. My face was burning; I felt heat around my forehead and nose and just wanted to go into the ground because I felt so bad for my brother and had no idea where he had gone.

I was scared of my father's rage after that, but he was by far less damaging than my mother. Children of narcissists instinctively feel the danger, even without understanding the workings behind the narcissistic behaviour. Despite her claims of love and the fact I needed her approval, I was sensing the childish, reactive, and unforgiving nature of my mother.

An example:

One summer evening, while visiting my mother's grandparents in their village, the creepy adult son of the neighbours had a good feel of my small breasts over my T-shirt. My reaction was the usual freeze, but I figured that he'd had a bit too much to drink and that there were other people not far away and he wouldn't dare do anything else.

I did not mention this incident to anybody. I knew what he did was wrong, but I knew the real danger if I said anything was at home. Even at the age of ten I had a good understanding of what was going to happen.

If I said anything, it was going to come right back to me. It was a small village, the neighbours knew each other and needed each other, and I was going to be the reason for possible tension. As an empath, I loved my grandparents and I did not want them to suffer because of me. My grandparents were close with their neighbours, and I did not want this to change because of some dirty thing.

Yet I knew my mother's devaluation was going to be the hardest to handle. I knew I was going to get that heavy look, the 'see, all this is because of you' and 'you are so not worth it' look. I felt it in my bones that she was going to turn any outcome against me. I wasn't worth any trouble if I was not a joy. Being a problem made me a target for my mother, and that was more unpleasant than having my breasts fondled by a drunk man.

Only victims of narcissistic parents can understand what is so disturbing about this example. Victims of narcissists have such low self-esteem they end up lost and reactive to others. It is a fundamental damage to the self-protection needed in life as a human being. Self-esteem is not only a protection, but a driving force and enjoyment in life. It gets badly worn down around narcissists, and their children have serious issues because of it.

DYNAMICS IN ABUSIVE FAMILIES – SUMMARY

The way to maintain good mental health is to stop the bad things getting to you. In dysfunctional families the blame is passed down to the weakest members. The bully parents do that directly and spontaneously as they lose control. With the covert narcissistic parents, passing the blame is a process driven by the narcissistic disorder. It is part of the narcissistic projection.

NARCISSISTIC PROJECTION

Projection is a major function of the narcissistic shell. Anything the narcissists don't like about themselves is projected onto others in order to keep their false image intact.

Part of the projecting is accusing their children of being exactly what the narcissistic parent is. Things like being selfish, for example. It is a major feature of the narcissists, but they accuse their children of it because they know what it is and are very afraid their children might not serve them as they are expected to. It is what they are most afraid of: that you will not put them first, as they believe they deserve.

The one thing my mother was instantly reacting to was any perceived sign of selfish behaviour, and she was attacking it with urgency and contempt.

PASSIVE-AGGRESSIVE COMMUNICATION

Passive-aggressive communication is the very opposite of good communication and it is used by narcissistic parents a lot. There is a whole array of techniques – withholding information, slander, minimising, double-binding, metalanguage, and so on.

My mother used metalanguage that conveyed dislike and disgust so she could not be accused of anything directly. She kept the illusion going that she was a good mother, and though I could sense her negativity, no one outside of the family could point to any abuse.

Passive-aggressiveness works well when the narcissists are in a position of power. Not so much when they are not. Unfortunately, they are in a position of power over their children.

MINIMISING

Minimising is abuse that does not leave visible scars. It is abuse, because it causes degradation and regression and the victims suffer long-term consequences.

Not acknowledging their feelings and their needs, undermines the personhood of the children. My mother did it by mocking, or by refusing to acknowledge that my problems mattered.

For example, when I was told I needed urgent surgery my mother was upset and vocal about it. 'Surgery? Do you know how dangerous that is? To cut you open ... People die from those gases they use ...' She went on and on in her 'I have to suffer so much because of you' manner. Not for a second did it occur to her that I was the one having the surgery and maybe I needed some reassurance.

She thought that acting upset is exactly what a good mother does. Of course a good mother will try to comfort a child, but mine did not, or could not. Either way, she made my state of mind worse. What I did not do was tell her to stop trying to scare me, because by then it was a matter of fact that my feelings did not matter.

DIFFERENT RULES

All adult children of narcissistic parents know this one: there are different rules for you and for the rest of the world. What is funny and adorable in others is negative in you.

For example, just the mentioning of contact lenses got my mother gasping in disbelief that I would dare to ask for such a thing. Later, she was saying how charming and interesting a new woman with contact lenses at work was.

In the same fashion, there are different rules for you and for them. My mother was not an achiever, she didn't do any sports, could not swim or drive, but she managed to make me feel like a failure about each of those things at different stages. She was quite plump, but I was quickly attacked for putting on any weight. She was never a success at work, so none of my achievements were ever acknowledged.

NARCISSISTIC NEGLECT AND/OR SMOTHERING

Narcissists can be smothering when it's convenient, and neglectful when some effort is expected and there is nothing for them in it.

My mother was not keen on dealing with any medical issues I had. With the exception of the seaside in summer, where my mother would be smothering me, she showed very little interest in where I went, what I did, or how I felt. The control came thick and fast only when she suspected she was losing her grip over me.

SABOTAGE

Sabotage is a major tool, it is an essential technique for making you, their children, feel inferior. Because covert narcissists are static, they do not try new things, and they do not like you to do so. And because they are not very good runners, so to speak, they will break your legs in order to stay ahead and be in charge.

The message is 'you will not get far without me.' This is why the narcissists sabotage their children, to prevent them from getting enough self-esteem to start noticing the shortcomings of the criticising parent.

Narcissists do that without any guilt or remorse. In their heads they can twist anything to serve their image. In this context, their entitlement over their children has no limits. They take from others as they breathe. They have a toddler's assumption that everyone owes them, everything is about them, and they are somehow deserving of the best.

Narcissistic parents sabotage by making any failure worse and by attacking the character of the children, while minimising any successful achievements.

An example:

I tried to learn to play the guitar. I had no musical talent and I struggled with it. When I stopped taking lessons my mother was triumphant and nasty about it. 'I knew it. You never finish anything ...' Someone else might have said, 'At least you tried ... It is good to try new things. This is how you find what you are good at and what you are not.'

Not the covert narcissist. If you are a child of one you will be familiar with the narcissistic smirk. It shows contempt, satisfaction, and self-righteousness because they knew you'd fail. It comes from a miserable place inside, from the jealousy and frustration that they don't get more out of life because they are simply entitled to more than you.

My mother didn't have any hobbies aside from complaining how hard her life was and how she was doing everything for us. This was not true at all, but she talked about it so often I believed she was the hard-working, suffering, and unfortunate one, and we were not appreciating what she was doing.

Back then, I knew nothing about covert narcissists. In retrospect, if I had succeeded at learning to play the guitar like a pro my mother would've been a lot angrier and dissatisfied. As an adult I learned to drive, travelled the world, and had a good job. That did not make my mother happy one bit, and in response she tried to take me down by attacking my hair, my weight, and my character when I was down. Covert narcissists are very skilled at using your weaknesses and the invisible wounds they have created to keep you down.

Another example of sabotage:

My father wanted me to do sports so somehow I ended up doing athletics. My coach, who I'd been trying to please and impress, came to talk to my parents about my future and the possibility of going to a certain school because of my athletic abilities.

After a short exchange, my mother shut the door in his face. I was confused and deeply embarrassed, because he'd made the effort to come and talk to them and he was not even invited in. I was the one who had to face him next time. In my child's mind, the behaviour of my mother was my responsibility.

The idea of me doing sports was my father's, not my mother's or mine, yet I was confused because I did not even get noticed for doing so well. 'You don't want to go there, do you?' was the only thing my mother said. She had that face with the sulky smile. I don't know what my father thought.

I got sort of lost after that. I carried on trying to impress my coach for a while, then ran out of energy. He lost interest in me as well. As I grew up and started dieting my athletic abilities declined sharply.

DOUBLE BINDING

The worst damage to the psyche of the children of abusive parents, is done by an abusive technique known as double binding.

A double bind is being trapped in a situation in which an individual is given two messages by someone with control and power over them, and one message contradicts the other.

An example is the narcissistic parent demanding that you please and achieve to win love, but constantly pointing out to you that you are weak and flawed. You cannot win that love and approval, because you are not meant to. They want you to achieve, but never admit your achievements. When you get close, the rules change, and you are not in a position to do anything about it.

Basically, the parent makes you feel faulty and inadequate, but wants you to perform and make them look good, which is very hard when you feel faulty and inadequate. They are keeping you back but wanting you to achieve and take care of them at the same time.

It is because the covert narcissists must have one up on you to keep the illusion they are so much better and morally superior. As long as they are seen as better, the narcissistic image is safe.

Similarly, when a narcissistic parent tells you they love you, but hurt and humiliate you at the same time, it messes with the very idea of what love is and creates future intimacy and relationship issues.

Likewise, saying one thing but expressing something else with their metacommunication, is a way of messing with your head, while the narcissist claims innocence and the high moral ground.

Growing up in such a toxic environment, and the repeated effect of the double bind, makes the children of narcissists lose hold of reality and turn to self-destruction and self-hatred.

SLANDER

Narcissistic slander is the covert way narcissists put you down in front of friends, relatives, and associates. They play the good-as-gold parent who expresses concern about how confused, or difficult, or bad their children are.

If you are a child of a covert narcissist you probably don't know the half of it, because it's done behind your back. I only found out the extent of it as an adult.

By undermining you they make sure that if you complain about the narcissistic parent nobody will believe you, because they already have a certain negative image of you. Again, this abusive behaviour is just how narcissists live day to day. The plotting and manipulation is necessary to twist others around their false image.

For people who claim to be good and so very moral, they play the most appalling games, like slandering family members in front of other family members without a second thought. Somehow they justify this in their heads, because everything is secondary to the need to keep seeing themselves as their disorder demands.

KEEPING CHILDREN SCARED AND NAÏVE

Covert narcissistic parents want to keep their children naïve and insecure so that they do not outgrow them. Their parenting does not provide any guidance or meaningful advice for their growing offspring. The end game is to make the children feel they cannot fend for themselves and believe they are lost without the parent.

An example:

My mother never talked to me about the fact that all women menstruate. I found out in the school's bathroom at the age of twelve. I went into a state of quiet shock, then the dots connected in my head – things girlfriends had giggled about that I could not understand made sense.

I went home and my mother confirmed this is what happens to all women. She did not look comfortable talking to me and she was slightly angry. I assumed I'd had my period way too early, and this is why she didn't tell me, or why she was unhappy. Twelve was the right age, I found out later on, but it did not take the shame out of the experience.

Talking about sex or menstruation cycles was a no-no. It was something dirty and too disgusting to talk about. Narcissists thrive in an environment of confusion and lack of information because they can trigger shame and emotional responses. Unfortunately, it is exactly what happened in my case. I was quite tall and I was the first one in my class to develop breasts, and it made me feel dirty and unpleasant. I ended up hating my growing body because it was giving me so much trouble and shame.

Narcissistic parents want you to be physically healthy but naïve and dependent, so that they have influence over you. Looking back, aside from manipulation, my mother wasn't exceeding in anything else. Mothering was her excuse, the 'looking after everybody' and 'doing everything for her children.' In her head, she was always going to be in charge of her children and grandchildren. That family control is what covert narcissists count on, because it's within their grasp.

The only thing my mother wanted was a 'good girl,' not someone able to stand up for herself out in the world. This is why my ability to cope was not a consideration. Destroying my self-esteem was just part of the game, as well as the scare tactics and constant reminders that life in general was very hard indeed.

ERODING YOUR BORDERS

Children of covert narcissists become empaths. In order to stay on the good side of their narcissistic parents they have to learn to empathise pretty early on. They put themselves in the shoes of others automatically, out of habit or because they feel threatened and empathising is what they do as a defence.

An example:

As a child at school, I felt for any troubles my parents, classmates, and friends had, and I was worried sick about global warming, about the forests disappearing and the endangered animals. All these issues were creating a physical reaction in me. I had no protective borders, no ways of stopping bad things affecting me.

You might think these issues are something to worry about, and they are, but there is a difference between having social responsibility and having cringing tension and pain in your stomach.

If you have a strong sense of self you can defend yourself and your beliefs. Having a fragile sense of self leaves you open to anyone to affect you in any way they want. It makes you dependent on others and is very much an illness. Borders are necessary for any person.

If you identify with this – if you took on the world's problems as a child, if you felt responsible for the well-being of your parents and just about everything else under the sun – please understand that was not normal. Your childhood was the foundation for your bad mental health and struggles through life.

Your sense of self was eroded in the dysfunctional family the same way your borders were. Making good things look bad is easy enough to do. The narcissistic parent targeted your major qualities and made them look bad. You assumed you are not likable and tried to hide and change those things that were a major part of you.

A good mental health rule is to make the best out of your strengths and learn to manage your weaknesses so you minimise their impact on your life. A good parent would teach their children how to cope best with what they've got.

The narcissistic parent does the very opposite – magnifies all your weaknesses and uses them to push your buttons and dig into you when they need to control you.

THE RESULT OF THE NARCISSISTIC ABUSE

To summarise, the children of covert narcissists are conditioned to feel inferior.

You are meant to be looking after their emotional and physical needs for life, while the control remains theirs. Every day small put-downs erode your self-esteem. Loosing self-esteem makes you regress, once you regress you depend more on the narcissistic parent, and they get angrier and angrier because you are the one that is supposed to look after them.

This is the double bind of the narcissistic disorder. They want you to do well for them, but they end up destroying you so badly you cannot even function like a normal person, never you mind doing well.

The narcissistic disorder is not providing solutions for the narcissist; it is about twisting reality in order to provide narcissistic supply.

Unfortunately, their children are the main victims of their disorder. The voice inside them becomes negative and demeaning, much like the narcissistic parent.

NARCISSISTS AND FAMILY RELATIONSHIPS

Covert narcissists, as the name implies, hide their agenda under pretences. They are not brazen enough to shout abuses or hit their children openly after they reach a certain age, or anyone else for that matter. Instead they use passive-aggressive behaviour to get their way.

An example:

My mother had control over her parents but not over my father's parents. They owned the flat we lived in, and the summer house. They were teachers by trade and people not easily manipulated.

By the time I was entering my teenage years my mother had managed to get them out of their own flat and managed to disrupt their relationship with my father and us. Over time the passive-aggressive narcissist can achieve anything. They are as creative and as determined as substance abusers, and they want what they want.

After my grandmother died I had fits of unbelievable guilt and kept on going to her grave. As a depressed, self-absorbed teenager I had failed to visit her while she was ill. After she died I remembered how good she was to me when I was a child and I felt a gut-wrenching sadness.

OTHER RELATIONSHIPS

To find out who the narcissists really are you have to ignore their self-promotion and their words and look into the relationships they have. There are ways to recognise a covert narcissist just by looking at their relationships.

My parents did not have many friends. As a kid I thought it was because of my unsocial father, but why my mother had nobody to complain to but me, was a mystery.

In fact the narcissists have a limited number of people they can have as friends, people who would provide supply and not challenge them. They do not like normal people, and normal people do not put up with narcissists.

This is why covert narcissists are not a danger to anyone with good borders. You have to be an empath and to have certain weaknesses that allow the narcissist to manipulate you. They are predators, because they use such people for their own purposes. Once they stop giving supply they get discarded with a drastic attitude change. Narcissists are very toxic people, and unfortunately their children are their biggest victims.

For example, one of the two families my mother kept in contact with was a couple bitterly complaining about their daughter who wanted to be an artist. My mother was taking all the sordid details in and was talking about it afterwards. Their problems diverted the attention from her own dysfunctional family.

The other couple liked complaining about life as much as my mother, and had similar views on who was to blame – everybody but them, of course.

There were no friends of my mother's that were happy with their lives and with their children, they had to have problems so her own family didn't stick out and look bad.

...

Another reason narcissists do not get to keep many friends is that their lack of empathy can lead to major slip-ups.

An example:

One summer, my mother met a woman at the seaside who she knew from somewhere. The woman was there with her husband and two small boys. The older boy had darker skin, and the younger was whiter. My mother was admiring the younger boy and saying how uncommon he was, and pushing the other boy away without bothering to control the expression of dislike on her face.

My mother was a racist, and that was because she thought of herself as a 'white woman,' and as such she assumed she was better by design. That 'status' made her special in her head, and it was irreversibly implanted in her personality. There was no logic or sense in that, just a belief that formed a part of her false image.

Openly disliking one of the children, as you might expect, did not go down well with the parents. The woman was good-natured and she was laughing at my mother's behaviour, but we never saw them again, as with many other one-time acquaintances.

I was eight or nine, but I had more empathy and understanding and felt embarrassed while my mother remained completely clueless. The narcissist's level of awareness and ability to read complex emotions is at toddler level, yet they have worked out how to mimic and fake good character.

It is a well-learned skill because it is the way covert narcissists make their way in the world without any real skill and capability – by projecting an image that makes others believe they are those special, important, irreplaceable people. The members of their families become enablers – people playing the narcissistic game. Yet those major mistakes they make are shocking and they do eventually destroy the illusion they are projecting.

NARCISSISTS – ARE THEY BIGOTS?

The 'strong' opinions of bigots are enforced with a deep fear of change and suspicion towards anyone that is not like them. Part of it is being raised with old-fashioned values and a lot of shame. This is why they are so reactive to anybody not sharing their values.

Narcissists are similar, but there is one difference: they do not truly believe in anything. The values are a cover, a representation of high moral values. The one and only priority is getting supply and keeping the false ego.

If there is a supply to be found, a covert narcissist will get close to a person that a bigot will never get close to on principle, and will do what narcissists do best – feed their ego through him or her. To justify their behaviour and keep their values they will come up with some excuse that makes that one person different than the rest of their kind.

Aside from keeping up appearances, narcissists do not have principles. They can shamelessly pretend in order to 'hook' a new source, and change their stance on things so quickly it will spin your head around.

Yet no matter how good they pretend to be, their lack of humanity comes through. Sooner or later people close to them figure out what they are truly like.

An example:

This is an example I witnessed later in life, but it illustrates perfectly the true lack of humanity people with the disorder have.

I witnessed it as an adult in my twenties, but it is a very clear example. My mother's cousin had a mentally underdeveloped grandchild; his brain had ceased to develop at the age of two though he was ten years old. She talked about him in the same way she talked about her other two grandchildren. The family had accepted the issue and was dealing with it the best way a caring family could.

While listening to her relative talk, my mother had a face of disgust and disbelief. She simply failed to register the pitfalls of letting her true feelings be known.

Moments like these are what give the narcissists away. Their brain mimics normal communication, but truly there is no humanity behind it.

It made me wonder why she was so disgusted by a handicapped child, someone else's child at that, someone she was not directly involved with at all.

I am not a psychologist, but what I find fits well is the presence of a very primal anger in the mind of my mother. It translates into something like, 'you are not supposed to get what I don't get.' The anger is there because someone like her cousin's grandchild could get attention and recognition, the things my mother thought she should get.

Narcissists think they are so special that everyone should see that and acknowledge that, and not pay compliments to those obviously beneath them. That kind of primal, blind anger and jealousy is experienced by people with stunted emotional development, with early childhood problems that were never dealt with in a mature way.

In this case, my mother failed to lie simply because she could not see complexities outside her own web and her needs, especially when occupied with some agenda of her own.

This raises another question:

WHAT CAUSES THE NARCISSISTIC DISORDER?

There seems to be an agreement in the academic sources that narcissism forms very early on. It sounds plausible; whatever damage my mother suffered it stopped her emotional development at a young age.

There is a lot written about the possible reasons for it, or what kind of experiences and traumas make people develop a narcissistic disorder. I can only speculate, of course, but this is what I know of my own mother that might explain what happened:

One thing she let out about her childhood was that she was 'a toy in her parents' hands.' My mother told me this while explaining to me what a good mother she was for letting me choose what to wear, but the switch of tone and expression showed deep anger and frustration.

She was the only child and, I am assuming, the focus of their lives. It's likely they expected her to be everything desirable in a child. She was praised for her looks that were fashionable at the time and she had a special status as their pride and joy, and she was not allowed to be imperfect as all humans are.

Idealising a child is abuse as well. Impossibly high standards no one can live up to, do not allow for normal development. What I read into it is that she was probably expected to be exceptional and special, and shamed when she failed to be so. That is a method of abuse because kids must be okay with who they are.

And so the dysfunction continued from one generation to another – the shame got passed along like a hot potato. And again, shame does not need to be justified. It is an unpleasant, humiliating feeling inside. My mother was fulfilling her parents' needs. She was probably not allowed her own feelings, and her real personality got lost in favour of the false image she had to project to meet expectations.

The hard shell of narcissism is there to protect a badly shamed core. Exposing it would be very painful, and even unacceptable, to a narcissist. So they decide to be faultless at any cost. And yet they are very good at shaming and judging others because they need to project onto others the things that endanger their perfect image.

I assume my mother's human nature – her imperfections and mistakes – were harshly punished when she was very young. I do not know. As far as I could observe, my grandparents were serving my mother's needs, not the other way around. She had taken control and was not about to let go. And maybe all that frustration of being a controlled child was at the bottom of her desire for control.

Maybe, maybe not. Remember, if you are a victim of narcissists do not ever feel sorry for them. What they are doing to you is far worse. The narcissistic parent can make you suffer like nobody else can, because they diminish, exploit, and devaluate without any remorse.

My narcissistic mother had the emotional maturity of an angry child that wanted to be seen as special and good, no matter what she did, and wanted to be the one in control. Yet the way to get that was through undermining and through sick head games.

Covert narcissists are vulnerable to stress and to self-doubt, and their insecurities are easily triggered if someone catches them out. The need to be validated is driving them to destroy those under them in order to be the one who is both better and better off.

Narcissists do not try to change, instead they work hard to keep the illusion they are perfect as they are, to manipulate the environment to fit what is in their own heads. This is energy consuming and never works completely. My mother had a well-hidden rage inside her, and when it came out it was pretty ugly.

NARCISSISTS VERSUS SELF-LOVING PEOPLE

There are people that love themselves unconditionally, no matter what. You have probably come across such people in your life – those who are happy with who they are and what they do, and seem to be surprisingly okay with their flaws.

Such people puzzle and sometimes annoy people with no self-esteem, because they seem to have it in great excess. Yet such people are not narcissists, because they don't need to be validated by you or anyone else. They don't try to manipulate others. They don't have the anger and malice when they don't get what they think they deserve, as the narcissists do. They are self-sufficient and rather happy people, to my view.

DISNEY MYTH ABOUT FAMILIES

Saying all mothers are good is like saying all people are good. Any sensible person understands this is not the case. Some parents are damaged and needy and they use and abuse their children. The parents themselves lack that very important ability to self-reference.

In society now, the status of the mother is special, and the love of the mother is considered one of the greatest things out there. It is so in most cases, but this works against the small section of victims of abusive mothers.

If you are one, you have to understand your parent is just a person, and not a nice one at that. They do not have any special rights over you. Abuse is abuse, no matter who does it.

You have to learn to ignore all those 'do-gooders' that will try to put you down because 'your poor mother loves you.' This is generalising, and a form of brainwashing. You know it in your heart. You do not owe anything to abusers.

HOW NARCISSISTS BUILD THE IMAGE OF 'GOOD PEOPLE'

Narcissists build the image of themselves as 'good people,' with words. If you wonder why they talk so much and never listen, it's because they narrate their experiences to make them relevant and to affirm their image. Or it might be that they don't like silence because it's reflective, and not something a narcissist can handle.

But there is a lot more to it. Talking is their strong point, their skill, their main tool of manipulation. The narcissists use it to build an image of themselves as 'good people.'

An example:

I recall my mother talking about the cleaning woman at her office, how she'd lost money on a scam and how worried she was. Listening to her tell the story, one might assume my mother cared about the woman and her problems. Why would she talk about it otherwise?

When my grandmother lost money on a scam years later there was no sign of any compassion. My mother treated her with anger and contempt. When the issue is close to the narcissist there is no understanding or compassion. Talking about the problems of others is just that.

Narcissists don't get affected by the problems of others in the negative way empaths do. Yet they need an audience, because the narcissistic shell needs to be reinforced by some sort of interaction with the world. Their opinions must be listened to, their ways must be acknowledged as better, and even their fears and worries must overshadow those of the others.

If they are not listened to in the family, the narcissists create an atmosphere of distress and uncertainty because it allows them to magnify the issues of the other members. They take sides between them as it's needed to assert themselves. Sometimes they create drama to serve that purpose, and show themselves as the heroes that have the answers to the drama they created in the first place.

The need of the narcissists to get their validation from their environment, is their undoing. The disorder works against them the more time goes by, but in the process they take down everyone they can get their hands on.

CHILDHOOD ROOTS OF COMPLEX PTSD

Most people know Post Traumatic Stress Disorder (PTSD) as a condition of soldiers and of people that have experienced extreme, life-threatening situations. The complex version is a result of trauma as well, but the reasons and the triggers are not as clearly defined.

It develops because of prolonged trauma in childhood. Feeling unloved, insecure and inadequate, not knowing how to look after yourself, not having borders, constant anxiety – all of it factors in. The trigger could be something as normal as intimacy or social situations, or everyday things that had become negative experiences.

A cause might be a prolonged low level of stress, but because it is unavoidable and unpredictable it wreaks havoc with the endocrine system and the body's healthy reaction to stress. The communication in the narcissistic family is inadequate and inconsistent, anxiety is always present in the lives of the children, and many develop Complex PTSD as adults.

The way the children learn to communicate with themselves and others is dysfunctional as well. This is the problem that stays long after they have left the family. Unfortunately, the signs of co-dependency can become such a part of the person that they don't even understand this is a disorder that can be fixed.

Common signs are constant tension in the muscles, shoulders, chest, arms, clenched hands, clenched jaw, teeth grinding, fear of socialising and speaking up, and many other signs that I will come back to later in the book.

WHAT I WOULD TELL THE CHILD INSIDE ME

This is what I would tell the child inside me:

I am sorry you were never loved. Love, as parental love, should feel good, safe, and uplifting. If it felt like someone was repeatedly kicking you in the stomach, it was abuse and not love. If you felt empty, alone, and bruised inside, you were not loved. As a rule, people who love you do not demean you.

As a child you did not know what covert narcissists were, yet you could sense the dysfunction in your family. Unfortunately, the abuse started so early you could not identify it as such. It was simply the reality you were in, and – as children often do – you ended up blaming yourself.

Another unfortunate thing was that you learned to keep your feelings inside and not ask for help because your problems were ridiculed.

You have to make peace with all of that. It wasn't your fault and you were not in a position to do anything about it. But you survived, you kept your personality and values no matter how torn and shattered, and that makes you stronger than any narcissist.

PART III: Covert Narcissistic Mothers and Teenagers

As you can probably guess, entering puberty does not make the lives of children in the narcissistic family any better. It's way worse on several accounts.

The children are no longer cute little things tickling the narcissistic ego. They are the opposite – moody and self-absorbed, trying to cope with body changes and with new interactions in the new social context they find themselves in.

This is when the children need a patient and supportive parent. This is when the narcissists are at their worst. No meaningful relationship between a parent and a child can be based on the demands of personality disorders and dysfunction.

As we already established, the narcissists need supply and validation, but give none back. After conditioning you to think that nobody would love you like your family, they will turn against you in your hour of need.

The long-time, unspoken agreement they hold you to in their heads is that your purpose is to agree and mirror their false image and hold them in high esteem, instead of becoming your own person.

Most teenagers are self-absorbed as they have a lot to deal with during this stage of life. It angers the narcissists a great deal and their attitude towards their 'bad' children changes into anger and irritation. Teenagers are trying to gain independence and find their way, and the game of the parent is to use their power in the family unit to sabotage and undermine their efforts.

The teenagers feel the change of attitude, but there is confusion as to why they suddenly get open dislike and disdain. Not understanding the narcissistic disorder and patterns of behaviour, they still think it's something to do with them.

And to a degree, it is. In many cases, by thirteen, the people pleasing, anxiety, and self-hatred have destroyed the child's energy and zest for life.

It was the case with me. I truly hated the puberty body changes and I had the strange feeling I was regressing, rotting away while my friends were flourishing and moving forward. Part of it was getting preoccupied with my own severe image problems and no longer providing supply for my mother. About this time, I stopped paying attention to her birthdays, and my mother's game changed drastically. She was no longer pretending she was a caring mother and became openly stroppy and critical towards me.

From age thirteen onwards my mother did not say anything good to me and maintained an angry and negative attitude. I was getting waves of dislike from her more often than not, and could feel her disdain for me in the way she gave me those long looks with the edge of her lip raised. She was disinterested and unhappy when I needed clothes or something for school, and I only dared ask for the necessities.

This is what makes the covert narcissists so caustic; they are there for the good times, gaining out of it, but when you are in need or in trouble they will abandon or attack you viciously instead of helping.

Even as a child, at some level I understood my mother was not good for me. Something was very wrong, and I felt so bad, like I was dying a little every day. By the time I was a teen I was worn down and bleeding from so many invisible wounds I was about to implode.

NARCISSISTIC PARENTS DO NOT CARE ABOUT YOUR PROBLEMS

An example:

At thirteen I realised that I needed glasses because I could not see the blackboard. My mother would not come with me, but she reluctantly gave me money for glasses.

I went alone to the optician. She kept on asking 'is this better or worse,' and I kept on saying 'better,' because I panicked and wanted to please her. She got more and more annoyed, and I am pretty sure I ended up with glasses that were wrong for me. The frames were thick and I almost never put them on, though I needed them to see properly.

This is a good example of how inconsistent narcissistic mothers are. The same woman who smothered me at the seaside could not care less about my eyes. She could not be bothered because my problems did not affect her directly.

Narcissists are unreliable and inconsistent parents simply because they are unreliable and inconsistent people. Their narcissistic shell is only concerned with the survival of their false image and getting narcissistic supply.

TEENAGERS AND SELF-DESTRUCTIVE BEHAVIOUR

The outcome of entering this critical stage with a distorted and minimised sense of self is predictable. Having no guidance on how to navigate the new challenges comes on top of not knowing how to cope with the old ones.

Not surprisingly, the teenagers like those amongst them who are secure and confident, and not the insecure ones. Self-esteem is critical in the way you present yourself. Knowingly or not, the teens seem to separate the 'cool' and 'uncool' on that account.

In my case, having no self-esteem and being tense and self-conscious made me uncool and my old friends moved away from me to keep their own status.

Unfortunately, back then I had no idea how to handle that. Much like my narcissistic mother, I expected my self-esteem to be lifted by something happening outside of me. Not at all like my mother, I had a false horrible image of myself, and not a false great one.

Without the healthy narcissism, the self-respect and the much needed self-care, I was unable to cope with rejection, and everyone gets rejected at times. My problems were snowballing without any solutions in sight. I was afraid to wear shorts, afraid my breasts were showing, always had huge, long T-shirts on – basically, I thought I was growing uglier and that others would notice if I did not cover myself. The challenges of growing up were simply beyond me. My sense of self was so distorted I had instant, unpleasant reactions to looking at myself in the mirror.

Once again, looking back I was a very normal looking teenager, with normal weight and size, with some good and some not so good features, but nothing at all that would justify such extreme behaviour or reactions. Nothing at all. It was the result of my mother's narcissistic campaign of distorting my reality.

The state I was in can be described as just waiting for the future to smack me in the face. The childhood zest for life was definitely gone. My girlfriends were embracing their bodies, fashion, and being teenage girls. Growing up was a struggle for me, and I felt left out and left behind.

SELF-LOATHING

This self-loathing is probably the worst damage done by the narcissistic parents, because from this point on the victims do the damage to themselves. The voice inside them is not loving or supportive, it is hateful and destructive.

I hated everything I thought I was becoming – fat, half-blind and uncool – and the more I hated myself the worse it got.

Most of my teenage years I was just trying to keep my head above water, there was no energy for fighting or defending myself, or challenging my narcissistic mother's toxic behaviour. Much later I found out this is a form of depression called dysthymia – mild depression that lasts for years. I was still functioning, but feeling constantly low, anxious and unhappy, and crying every single night.

At this stage I wanted something to change about the way I felt, but did not understand that this could only happen if I changed the way I felt about myself. There were many essential things I did not know, including what abuse was. I thought it was a physical thing.

Emotional abuse is as damaging as physical and sexual abuse, and it has the same long-term effects on the behaviour of the victim.

Emotional abuse makes you ashamed of who you are. It turns your life into a struggle in a twisted and unnecessary manner. Having a narcissistic parent and a dysfunctional family is like a chronic illness that sucks the life out of you. One term used in this context is 'negative conditioning': ignoring the good and looking for the bad.

An example:

My father did it in a direct way when annoyed, saying I had a big butt, big ears, bad posture. That did not happen often, but in the complete absence of positive things said about me the bad ones stayed with me.

My mother was angry and dismissive in a covert way. Angry I was dressing in black, angry I was wearing glasses, angry I was so unsocial, and annoyed when I was sick.

An example of a covert put-down is my mother saying to me, 'I saw Betty today. What a lovely, fresh girl she has become …,' while giving me a look with a microexpression of disdain. Using metalanguage was her way to humiliate me without doing anything anyone can hold against her.

This is how covert abuse works: by giving compliments to others she showed me she could indeed give compliments. By not ever giving compliments to me she showed me I was the one that was not deserving of any, and the only reason for it I could come up with was that I was substandard somehow.

This was the assumption throughout my entire childhood, though it was less obvious when I was little. I was undesirable by default, and I had to keep on defending my existence by pleasing. Of course that does not work in the long run; in the opposite – it is the foundation of bad mental health.

For good mental health it is extremely important to know your existence is not something you have to justify. Being born gives you the same rights to life as anyone. You are a unique being, and nobody has more or less rights to be alive. What you are given by nature or what position you have in society does not affect that fundamental human need.

This is a simple concept a lot of people with mental issues struggle with.

CHILDREN IN DYSFUNCTIONAL FAMILIES

In a dysfunctional family unit, the parents do not see their children as separate human beings. The children are 'theirs,' and somehow that translates into not having to show respect or put an effort into helping them build up their personalities for the children's sake.

The inherited connotation is that respect is something only the parents deserve and they do not have to justify why they do anything they do. This is an authoritarian attitude common in underdeveloped societies where the children are seen as a resource for the parents.

In a matter of speaking, dysfunctional parents are emotionally underdeveloped and they think their children can and should somehow be a resource, and should make them happier somehow. Of course, as mentioned before, children cannot solve the emotional problems of the parents. The opposite happens – the children become recipients of the parents' anger and negativity.

My father's worth was connected with his work, and when things went wrong he was stroppy and angry at home. It was pretty straightforward – he could not teach us how to cope because he was struggling himself.

With convert narcissists, the abuse is driven by the narcissistic disorder. In her need for supply my mother purposefully destroyed her family one by one to make herself look better. Once I could not be a supply for her, any parental responsibility – never mind love – got replaced with hidden malice and tactics that messed badly with my head.

This level of nastiness is only the domain of the narcissists and their disorder. They are the ones that sustain themselves the longest in the family, provided those around them remain enablers and co-dependents.

This is why learning about the disorder is so important for their victims.

CONSEQUENCES OF MENTAL TORMENT

Mental health is as important as physical health, but much less talked about. There seems to be a reluctance to state the obvious: mentally unfit parents cannot teach their children good mental health.

The narcissists are only concerned with their false image and making others acknowledge it. Their demise takes time and takes others down. The co-dependents they create have a false, negative image and expect circumstances and pleasing others to provide them with some self-esteem. Their demise is much quicker.

Both ways of trying to sustain the ego are sick and dysfunctional, and the consequences are damaging, both psychologically and physically.

A period of severe dieting got me seriously unwell at fourteen and lasted for years. The dieting and constant stress became a physical problem – anaemia and a serious thyroid issue.

Yet it seems the psychological issues presided over the physical. The bad place I was in led to some impulsive and dangerous behaviour.

An example:

I was waiting at a bus stop when a scrawny, bearded man came and started talking to me. He was maybe in his mid 30s. He was weird-looking, but he said he noticed I was special and offered to do a palm-reading.

I knew I shouldn't talk to him, but I did anyway because he told me I was special. He told me a wave of new people was coming, intuitive and paranormally gifted, that were going to rule in the new millennium.

Maybe, I thought, just maybe he did know of some secret society that would appreciate 'different' people like me. Maybe I had some hidden power. Maybe, miraculously, I'd start being and feeling better.

I was desperate for compliments, anything positive and helpful. I even went to his apartment, a simple place with so many books, all about physics or psychics. He spoke in a quiet, intelligent manner, and he didn't try anything funny on me at first. He did, in the end, suggest that we should get married and that I should pay more attention to my posture. That's when the bells started ringing in my head; I took off and stopped any contact.

It haunted me for a while, though – the fact I was so stupid and not special at all. I was just as weird as he was.

Looking back at this story I understand why self-esteem and respect are so important. Without self-respect, one makes bad decisions, and dangerous ones at that.

Knowing what I now know, I understand I was unable to perform mental health related functions that most of my peers could, like self-soothing, self-championing, and self-respect. Those are necessary for good mental health. Respecting yourself is making good choices. Self-hatred makes people do the craziest things.

In a healthy person, the validation comes from inside – knowing who you are and being okay with it, is there. Children of narcissists do not have much of a chance, but not all is lost – they can learn to do some of it as adults.

PHYSICAL MANIFESTATION OF NARCISSISTIC ABUSE

Over time, the continuous anxiety becomes more evident in the physical state of the children of narcissistic parents. The symptoms are extensions of those from childhood – tension, fatigue, shallow breathing. Those are general signs of abuse. They include clenching one's fists and jaw when in social situations, shaky voice, avoiding eye to eye contact, concentration problems, lack of borders, and an inability to handle strong emotions.

An example:

In my case, the constant dieting was a factor as well, and I struggled to walk up hill. On a family weekend out, I was trying so hard to keep up I felt sick and ended up vomiting on the side of the track.

I was so ashamed that I did not mention it to any of my friends. If I had, I might've gotten good advice from someone, like to get a check-up. Apparently, my parents were not worried about me being sick, because they did not suggest any such thing. My sickness was nothing but a failure of character, and instead of being concerned both were acting disappointed and smug at the same time.

To this day I cannot entirely comprehend why my failures were so satisfying to my parents. Maybe they felt safe in their authority over someone so much weaker than them.

Later, it turned out that I had severe iron deficiency and needed urgent thyroid surgery. Of course nobody acknowledged that was the real reason for my declining abilities, and the negativity and humiliation remained with me.

Dysfunctional parents do not apologise. It is one feature that the children of narcissists would instantly agree on. They will lie and justify themselves, but never accept they did anything wrong.

Looking back, I see how desperate for approval I was and how hard I tried when there was no chance I was going to please my parents. Because of my toxic, narcissistic upbringing it took me two years to get surgery and more than twenty years to understand what was really happening to me. The main reason for it was the covert way my narcissistic mother managed to twist my reality.

…

Another physical manifestation of narcissistic abuse is in the posture and the body language of the victim. Typically, it's unusual tension and stillness. The state of discomfort is the result of being shrunk inside, being in a state of perpetual shame and fear that you will be further ridiculed and shamed. The default settings of children in narcissistic families are set to shame and dysfunction, and that is the reason they are troubled adults and suffer a great deal.

When you are stressed and helpless, the body produces adrenaline and other related hormones until exhaustion eventually sets in. It is the beginning of depression and the related issues later in life.

Those are signs of abuse in general. More specific to the narcissistic abuse, for example, is the inability of the victims to accept compliments.

CHILDREN OF NARCISSISTS AND COMPLIMENTS

Children of narcissists are not only not used to it, but they react negatively to compliments. It's because it clashes with their internal beliefs of unworthiness and makes them uncomfortable. It's an emotional reaction, but often the whole body responds. Something inside screams foul play and the reaction is tension and awkwardness at the 'intrusion' of the compliment.

The result is feeling like a fraud that has managed to mislead someone, but that the truth is bound to come out. Being complimented becomes a source of pressure and a burden.

This is part of the learned behaviour of self-sabotage. Being liked is not a likely or sustainable concept for the children of narcissistic parents.

It seems the brain, as complex as it is, has a primal wiring that is very reactive, and it uses reactions to the environment that are learned through repetition.

After narcissistic abuse, the brain assumes negativity is fair play but struggles with positivity. It caches every slip but ignores the good. And it assumes you are the target of everyone's bad moods.

NARCISSISTIC GASLIGHTING

Narcissistic gaslighting is a major tool of manipulation. It's about distorting your perceptions and asserting what works better for the abuser.

An example:

At fourteen, a lump on my thyroid gland was clearly visible and it was bothering me so much I went to the local clinic. A doctor said I would probably need surgery and told me to get my parents to take me to a specialist.

I tried, but my mother could not be bothered with doctors and she gave me a necklace with some stone on it that was supposed to get rid of my thyroid problem. It didn't, my voice was getting dull, and the ends of my hair were splitting. I had a problem with the skin on my eyelids, it was peeling away in big patches and getting caught on my eyelashes.

I thought it was a problem, but my mother said my eyelids had always been like that. I did not remember having such a problem before, I said, but she snapped. 'Of course you did. Do you know, or do I know?' It was a categorical statement, not a question.

This is an example of narcissistic gaslighting. The assumption was that I was crazy or acting up, and that the problems were in my head. The problems with my hair and voice were once again deemed a failure of character: I was simply the way I was and nobody could do anything about it.

The gaslighting continued for two years while I was getting worse, till finally I managed to get my mother to take me to the doctor.

It turned out I needed urgent surgery, luckily just in time to prevent the loss of the entire thyroid. There was a cancer scare on the surgery table, and half of my thyroid got cut out. This information came from a nurse, not from my mother who did not say a thing about it to me.

Withholding of information is another form of gaslighting.

After the surgery my physical condition improved, but not my mental state. The gaslighting continued in another form – constant passive-aggressive attacks.

When it becomes clear the narcissists are wrong about something they go on the attack, throwing all sort of irrational blame and accusations to take the attention away from themselves.

My mother was lashing out at me for taking the medication I was given and for giving her such worries, and that was confusing. There was no acknowledgment of the fact I was sick, or even talking about how and why it had happened; there were only angry passive-aggressive digs at me about it.

Looking back, it's very strange that I never acknowledged how very little my problems meant to my mother.

Many adult children of narcissists wonder why they were unable to see their parents for who they were for so long. It's because the focus and blame had always been on them. It's the result of subtle, consistent gaslighting ever since they were born.

Abusers – narcissists or others – do not have the normal person's capacity for compassion and decency, this is why they abuse. Narcissistic parents can watch you unravel and do nothing.

It's easy to see this if you are a healthy person, but children of narcissists have distorted perceptions. If you have not been treated well all your life, how do you know what that is? The only chance the children have is to get away and to rethink the entire sick value system instilled in them.

NARCISSISTIC INJURY AND RAGE

The narcissistic, passive-aggressive assaults on you are meant to prevent you from judging them, among other things.

Narcissists cannot take criticism, and this is why they react with such fury when challenged. But there is something else that scares them even more, and it's being found out. If their hidden motivation is revealed it puts their image in mortal danger, and without the image the narcissist is nothing. There is no authentic self, it got lost in favour of the false image. Inside the shell is a lot of unresolved shame and denial.

This is why if you manage to shake their image you will get the narcissistic rage – a violent rage of a small child.

Seeing them for who they are enrages the narcissists, because they don't want to admit to the ugly mess that is inside them. No disorder comes from a good place. There is something very wrong at the bottom of it, but the narcissists would rather attack others viciously than admit they have a problem. The narcissistic shell 'repels' anything that is a danger to their false image.

This is why they constantly project negativity and criticism onto others. Prolonged exposure to narcissists causes mental paralysis in the victim – being attacked so many times causes you to shrink, to be always on the defence and to stay invisible. It is a state of not feeling right in your own skin.

COMPLEX PTSD AND INTIMACY

Trauma repeated for years and years, shows later in life as Complex PTSD. The long-term exposure to situations you had no control over, a chronic repetitive stress and entrapment, creates neuro-pathways in your brain firing together in reaction to specific events. For an adult child of a narcissist it feels like going back to a childlike state of helplessness and misery.

The trigger can be any social situation, being the centre of attention, being liked – any normal part of life. The reaction is very much due to the toxic shame instilled in you by the narcissistic parent.

In this context, even intimacy can be a trigger.

Because of the monumental betrayal of trust the covert narcissistic mother inflicts, the children end up thinking there is danger in trusting anyone who professes love. It triggers not only disbelief and an unpleasant gut reaction, but a whole set of brain responses. It's a knee-jerk reaction, because love is not a good thing in your reality. It exists only as a sort of movie idea or escapism.

Intimacy retriggers that devastating experience of betrayal. It's a very entrenched response, because the brain – and specifically the amygdale – responds in a mechanical way. Complex triggers register as danger because of the negative conditioning, and that is what the brain responds to because the need for survival overrides the rest.

As a teenager I used to sabotage any good relationship that came my way. As an adult, when my husband complimented or hugged me unexpectedly it provoked the physical reaction of wanting to cry, clenched jaw, muscle tension, or even anger. My mind expected it to be a set-up and a betrayal of major proportions.

Love, closeness – those are supposed to be good things, but they are connected with trauma in adult children of narcissists. This is why they often end up marrying other narcissists, because there is some comfort in the familiarity of the pattern.

FACING ADVERSITY

You have heard those stories the media loves so much about brave people facing incredible difficulties, facing illnesses, missing limbs, and thriving in the face of adversity.

If you are a child of a narcissist you might feel like such a wimp compared to them.

The truth is you don't have what they do – the will to live, confidence, self-belief, self-love and importance, or even the ability to ask for help when you need it – all the things that make you fight for your life and thrive.

That is exactly what the narcissistic parent has taken from you, the 'I am precious, I matter and I deserve to live' part. I assume the situation is much worse for children of narcissists who face additional physical or mental challenges as well.

The narcissistic parent made you focus on the negative and on your weaknesses, and think of them as your character.

PROCESSING REPEATED TRAUMA

The lack of love, security, and self-assurance, and the deep-seated feeling of inadequacy, translate into constant tension and constant release of adrenalin and other related hormones. The trigger is no longer any physical danger, but the everyday interactions children of narcissists struggle to cope with. An ancient part of the brain still reacts to those complex triggers as it used to react in life-threatening situations. It even reacts to recollections of stressful events, flashbacks of past bad experiences.

The one part of the brain that can overturn this reactivity in the long term is the frontal lobe and the repetition of a different way of thinking about yourself in relation to the environment.

You have to process and assess the perceived danger with your frontal lobe, with logic and reason, and remove the emotional fear response shamed into you by your mentally unfit parent.

WHY CHILDREN OF NARCISSISTS CANNOT HANDLE BEING LIKED BY OTHERS

Going back to the start of this book, if you are a child of a covert narcissistic parent you would be familiar with the inability to handle being liked by others.

This is one example illustrating the issue:

Everyone at school was crazy about a rock band and I had two photos of the frontman everyone wanted. By that time, I was avoided by most classmates because of my insecurities and other 'uncool' trends. A confident, younger kid I didn't know came up to me and started talking to me. Impulsively, I gave him the two photos, because I was so grateful that he decided I was worth talking to and I had to justify his trust in me somehow. My classmates were upset at me for giving the photos away and that was all that came out of my impulsive gesture.

Later in life, this pattern continued. Even as an adult I messed up a job I had to do for someone who openly praised my work. I panicked; I wanted to impress him so badly I did the exact opposite. This was not the behaviour of a healthy person, and now I understand the roots of it.

Not being able to accept compliments or cope with people who give you positive attention is a result of covert narcissistic abuse. It's an overwhelming feeling of being very grateful mixed with tension, panic, and fear that any positive attention is a trap and that rejection will certainly follow.

Children of narcissists have so little self-esteem that they are afraid if they lose the last of it there would be nothing to hold on to and they would find themselves falling into a bottomless pit. The fear unfortunately leads to more anxious self-sabotage and more self-loathing.

OTHER DIFFICULTIES

Any interaction with people is more difficult for children of narcissists. As a teenager, I used to buy clothes I didn't like just because I could not disappoint the shop assistants. Once they started talking to me I got into some sort of compressed, feverish headspace and I just could not walk out while they were looking at me. I had a deep fear of rejection, as if parts of me were crumbling down each time someone thought ill of me.

This was an extreme reaction, and looking back I realise I was in a seriously bad state. I was unable to complain about anything or even maintain eye contact with people. I had the mindset of a doormat.

At this stage I felt a huge resentment towards my mother that I could not put into words. I felt she was working against me and making my pain worse, yet I was not able to see the full impact and the patterns of abuse.

NARCISSISTIC PROJECTION

As mentioned above, anything that is unacceptable to the narcissistic image gets attributed to others. It is a subconscious transfer, it's a way of denying it's something they are doing or thinking because they accuse someone else of doing or thinking it. It's projecting their own mindset onto others, including their children.

Narcissists find in others things that they experience and know about, like jealousy, hatred, undermining, and – of course – selfishness.

An example:

My mother was very vigilant about me being selfish. Any perceived sign would get an instant reaction.

At one stage, I got into baking. I did bake for everyone, of course, not just for myself, but I was accused of being selfish because it was my idea and probably what I was doing was perceived as a challenge to my mother's 'turf.' Or probably because I was doing something I wanted to do.

Initiative is not what the narcissists appreciate. It is a red light. Somehow you are worthy only as an offsider, a presence, a listener, or an excuse when things go wrong.

My mother's reaction was covert, of course. It was in her crooked smiles and in her tone, as if I was doing something deserving of contempt. I heard her telling my father that I knew how to spoil myself, knowing that he hated the idea of spoiled children. So I stopped baking and it became one of the many faults my mother was accusing me off – not sticking with anything.

The accusations were painful because they weren't true; I wasn't spoiled, not by any standards. I was miserable. It seemed the more I tried to get some sign of approval, the more I failed – the second face of my mother was on most of the time, and I was the target of her passive-aggressive resentment.

Now I understand her classic narcissistic fear. My baking did not serve my mother's false image and, as such, it was seen as a selfish act. Looking after yourself would be very threatening to a narcissist. They need to be looked after first and always, and not compete for status.

Taking on interests is taking your attention away from them, and what you should be doing is listening, agreeing, feeding their ego, being their loyal sidekick. Their image is dependent on those around them, on the participation of the enablers. Their image must be seen and reflected back. This is why they had children in the first place.

Being accused of only taking care of yourself when you don't have a clue how to, and letting everyone walk all over you, messes badly with your head. Narcissists accuse you of being what they are.

As a survivor of narcissistic abuse I can look back at the numerous accusations thrown my way, from a different point of view. It was my mother who never finished anything simply because she never tried anything. Her false image demanded she was picture-perfect as she was. And because keeping up a false image is so energy consuming she didn't try new things and did not have hobbies or interests outside of the family.

PATTERNS OF THE NARCISSISTIC DISORDER

And here comes the real catch, the thing you have to understand about narcissists: everything you do or say is automatically about them. This is why having independent emotions is mocked. The only criterion that matters is how something benefits or disadvantages them and their false image.

To be a good parent, one has to have the ability to distinguish between their own feelings and their children's feelings, and the different places they are coming from. This is how good parents are able to teach better reasoning, which is more beneficial and mature in terms of the future challenges the children will face.

Mature parents want healthy, happy children who can deal with life, and they give them the tools to do well. The narcissists lack the ability to understand that they are the responsible party, not only for providing food and clothes, but for teaching children how to deal with their emotions and how to cope out in the world.

A parent capable of empathy would feel uncomfortable or worried if their kids suffer, but not the narcissistic parent. This is why they make things so much worse for their children. When you are miserable they can react with satisfaction as well as anger. This is when you catch the narcissistic smirk, a self-righteous satisfaction in being clearly better than you.

The anger comes from the fact you are not making their lives better despite 'everything they've done for you.' Instead you are sick and needy, and that is a great put-off for a narcissist. When they don't get their 'rewards' out of the children any longer, they become extremely angry and resentful.

Even at this point, the covert narcissistic parent will still try to deny any abuse and pretend they care despite the fact you are 'such an undeserving and ungrateful child,' so as they cannot be accused of being a bad parent. The illusion is very important to them, because they need to be in a position of high moral ground in order to use the empathy, co-dependency, and the good nature of others.

This is why the abuse is not likely to escalate past certain boundaries. They will not kick you out of the house or physically hurt you, not if you don't push them out of their comfort zone.

Narcissists do not let go of you easily because they have invested a lot of effort into making you an enabler. As long as you are in the family unit they need you, even if you are 'bad.' The interaction and your emotions are still something to feed on, and something is better than nothing. It appears narcissists are uncomfortable with silence and with being alone. The interaction is what makes them real. As long as you are around, you are a part of their games.

Another reason they do not escalate past certain boundaries is that they are afraid of being found out. Narcissists are only after supply. This is the drug, they are the addicts, and there is not much to be done about it. It's unlikely they will look for help, or accept they have any issues or faults.

WHAT HAPPENS WHEN YOU CONFRONT A NARCISSIST

If you confront a narcissist about their ways they will deny any wrongdoing and simply change the history to suit them. And it can have very bad consequences if you still depend on them.

Covert narcissists will not retaliate immediately. Manipulation is such a part of their existence that they will wait for you to make a mistake or set you up to make one to mask the true source of their anger, and then retaliate by making you look bad and attack your character.

An example:

As a teenager I confronted my mother about how poisonous the atmosphere was at home. She simply denied any of it was true with her usual expression, lips tight and chin up. Nothing happened for a couple of days, and then the mother of all shitstorms broke out.

What happened was my mother gave me permission to spend a night with a girlfriend. I thought that was strange, because it was the very first time I was allowed to spend a night away. The next day, I came home to find my mother fuming with self-righteousness, waiting to tear into me. She called me a homeless dog because I did not come home right away, and carried on attacking my 'loose' behaviour. It was a shock because I was used to her covert attacks and not full-blown open attacks, and it was so upsetting because my behaviour was anything but loose.

She had managed to set my father on me as well. He went with the traditional 'as long as you are under my roof you will follow my rules,' and I was never to spend another night away. He was very angry for someone who did not much care where I was, I can only guess what my mother had told him to make him so angry.

My head was spinning, my sensitive nature overreacting and making my whole body shake. I felt terrible, but back then I did not trace the attack to our talk a few days earlier.

This is how tricky covert narcissists are. The realisation came only after I learned about the way narcissists operate. Their methods are those of someone claiming the high moral ground to trigger that toxic shame in you.

All the brainwashing she did – all the 'mothers love their children' and 'nobody will care for you like your family' – was just part of her gaslighting campaign. This is an appalling behaviour from a parent, and if you are a victim of a narcissist you have to understand: It wasn't your fault. It was never your fault. It wasn't even about you. It was about your narcissistic parent, their disorder and their false image.

WHAT I TELL TEENAGERS WITH NARCISSISTIC PARENTS

This is what I tell teenagers with narcissistic parents:

Knowing and accepting you are human is important for good mental health. It comes naturally to others, but not to children of narcissistic parents. You have the right to experience your emotions, to make mistakes, to have weaknesses. It's all part of life. You do not have to justify your existence to anyone.

Being self-conscious is about always looking for your faults, trying to hide your faults, and being worried everyone will find out you are deeply flawed and will treat you like your narcissistic parent did. The truth is most people do not care about your flaws, and they have their own.

Being human is a messy business. Once you manage to wrap your head around the fact that your faults and imperfections are part of who you are, it will make you stronger. Work with what you've got, work on improving yourself, but do not beat yourself up for things you cannot change. Your internal voice should be kind and supportive. How you feel inside comes through.

As a child of a narcissist, what you are good at is empathising with people, so imagine you are a friend of yours and have compassion and patience for yourself and for the mental torment and distortion you've been through. Comfort yourself like a best friend would. It feels good being with someone positive and encouraging, someone who lifts you up instead of tearing you down.

Remember, compassion is the cure for toxic shame.

What you have been missing in your very core is the healthy and necessary narcissism that prevents bad things coming through and stops self-destruction.

Existing – being here and now – should be enough reason for you to enjoy life.

WHAT I WOULD TELL THE TEEN IN ME

This is what I would tell the teen in me:

I am sorry you were feeling so low and you lost so much time. There were so many cuts bleeding you, so much poison around that you could not possibly thrive in such an environment. I am sorry you ended up having so much hatred for yourself.

Yet you made it so far, and that says a lot.

Accept that your covert narcissistic parent was like a terminal disease. It wasn't fair, but bad things happen at random. And do understand that you did not have a choice. You adjusted to what was there because you had to. And even then you were stronger than the narcissist, because you kept your values and you never believed the false image. You can heal and bring back the joy to your life, and eventually you will, so hold on.

PART IV: Narcissists and Adult Children

If you didn't get the chance to learn any of the above as a teenager, it is likely you continued to struggle with bad mental health issues, and that the narcissistic parent continued to rule you and your life even when you were an adult.

Adult children of narcissists face a number of issues: Not knowing how to take care of themselves, inability to ask for what they need, low self-esteem, people pleasing, inability to face challenges and criticism, and so on. It is a long list. The constant anxiety is tiring, and without the ability to enjoy the little things life becomes difficult and bleak. This is why the victims of covert narcissists struggle.

As an adult, you might have learned how to deal with some of the issues in order to get through the day, but without understanding what the source of the problem was recovery would be unlikely.

The truth is that the healthy narcissism is critical for good mental health, and it is what you need to enjoy life. It is a fundamental human need – without it, anyone will eventually unravel.

Achievements and successes will not replace what the parent with narcissistic disorder destroyed in you. These things might make you feel better for a while, but will not fix the type of damage done.

An example:

I got a scholarship to one of the most prestigious universities in the country. For a while I was riding high on that, but in the second year the high wore off and I was unable to cope with my day-to-day existence. The next crippling depression had been coming for a long time, and was probably the logical extension of years and years of self-destructive thoughts, and was the start of alcohol abuse.

It got worse in spring. There was a heaviness in my head and in my body, a lack of energy and an overwhelming sense of melancholy. I remember being so very tired. It was sickness, but I was not able to recognise it. Back then, depression wasn't talked about and I had no clue as to what was happening to me. I was unable to concentrate and study, or even think straight. Yet I thought there was nothing to blame but myself, because I was very defective. I recall sitting on a bench for the longest time, not wanting to do anything or to face anything. I still managed to get up every time and keep on functioning, if only just.

NARCISSISTIC ABUSE AND DEPRESSION

One description of depression is anger turned inwards. There is more than one possible cause of depression, but this definitely describes one of them.

The victims know it in their bones that their condition is a result of something very wrong in their lives, something unfair and demeaning. Despite their best efforts to please, they were stripped of any value and joy. Yet they are unable to point to any severe case of abuse, because it happened subtly and over time, and they were brainwashed into blaming themselves.

Eventually they figure out what the source is, but in the case of the covert narcissist the world tells them they are wrong, and the brain struggles to deal with the additional gaslighting.

Children of covert narcissists know that the worse you feel the more the narcissistic parent will attack you. This is the reason they will suffer their whole lives if they don't get away. The episodes of depression are likely to repeat and get worse. It is hard to get up when someone is constantly putting you down, and a narcissistic mother will make you feel worse in your most desperate moments.

An example:

My mother's reaction to my depression was exactly what is expected from a covert narcissist. My 'badness' was faced with such passive-aggressive anger that one might think my mother was the only victim of my depression. She was bitterly and loudly disappointed her daughter turned out to be bad despite her motherly sacrifices.

First, she gathered the flying monkeys – some relatives that never cared to talk to me like a person before. This was followed by the silent treatment for weeks, which turned out to be a great relief for me.

After this period, my mother's attitude turned openly toxic. There was no more hiding her feelings in metalanguage. The illusion she was a good mother was broken irreversibly.

Sooner or later the true face of the covert narcissist comes out, the nasty angry side that is terrified of losing their influence and not getting what they expected to get from the children.

PEOPLE PLEASERS IN THE WORKPLACE

Once children of narcissists manage to move away from the narcissistic parent, things are likely to improve in the short term.

Unfortunately, as adults they carry the destructive abuse in their heads, the low self-esteem and the inadequacy instilled in them. Most are pretty broken and likely to struggle with the normal ups and downs in life that others can deal with.

How can you spot a people pleaser at the workplace? They are the ones that work hard, work holidays, help others, train new staff, and don't ask for anything in return. Often they are just thankful to get a job, and feel it's necessary to justify the trust put in them.

With time, resentment and bitterness builds up. While trying so hard, people pleasers do not succeed at work. They are passed over for promotions, and used by their colleagues and bosses simply because they make it so easy.

Because of their problems they do not always communicate efficiently and are not able to use their full range of abilities. And it's not a surprise that they burn out quickly and are likely to have repeated episodes of depression.

An example:

My first job was as a dishwasher in a small café. I worked as hard as I could, coming to work twenty minutes earlier and never asking the chef for lunch as the rest of the staff did. Only a child of a narcissist can understand how worthless and how undeserving of any effort one can feel. I had an overwhelming survival need to be liked, and there was a whole lot of anxiety generated around that.

While looking for a better job I met an employment agent, but as I was giving her my CV my hand shook violently and unexpectedly, triggered by my desperation to find a job and my fear of failure. After that my whole body went slightly wobbly and, of course, I never got a call from her. It was obvious I was in a bad way.

In time, I managed to recover to some degree, found a job, and moved away from my dysfunctional family. Life got better, but that was not the final solution to my mental health issues.

WHY CHILDREN OF NARCISSISTS STILL STRUGGLE AS ADULTS

Children of narcissists still struggle as adults because they struggle with so many issues, and because they haven't figured out the source and the nature of their illness, and the way to heal. Their default settings are set to self-hatred and self-sabotage, which makes them targets for narcissists and other predatory personalities out there.

Isolation is a major problem as well. Emotional abuse is not as widely and legally acknowledged as physical or sexual abuse. If someone with power over you kicks you in the stomach while you are on the ground, that's clearly abuse. If someone humiliates you when you are down again and again, you might just get the blame for it.

The mental anguish is self-directed, it's a learned affliction. It is a default setting because you have become the opposite of a narcissist – a sponge for all blame, shame, and negativity in your everyday interactions.

NARCISSISTS AND ADULT CHILDREN

Do you feel your parents treat you the exact same way as they did when you were a child? Do you feel exhausted, like you want to cry, depressed, and on edge every time you see them?

These are all signs that you are an adult child of a narcissistic parent.

You have regressed to a childlike state because of the years of abuse when you were most susceptible. This false programming of fear and inferiority was for the benefit of your parent, not you. When you feel inadequate, unsure, and helpless, you are open to manipulation and control.

The designated roles for the children do not change with time in the dysfunctional family dynamics. Getting married, or having your own children, or having success at work – it does not make any difference, because the issues are with the narcissistic parent and their enabling spouse, not with you.

In order for the dysfunctional family to function, the children must be playing the part assigned to them. If you are the Scapegoat, no matter what your achievements are your parents will not acknowledge them because it might change the established dynamics.

It's not difficult to put a negative spin on anything and bring people down, and the narcissists are experts at finding the negative and bringing their children down. If anyone wishes to look for the negative, they will find it, or make it up, or manage to tarnish the positive.

An example:

My mother would rather walk than be in a car with me. She could not make peace with the fact I was a driver. On the couple of occasions she was a passenger, she was tense and edgy, and that made me upset and tense. Her body language was that of mistrust in my abilities. There was no way she was ever going to admit I could be as good as any other driver on the road.

This is a good example of the narcissistic disorder. It does not always serve the person with the disorder, because it dictates irrational behaviour. No matter that I could drive, she'd rather walk or take the bus.

Such behaviour just adds to the daily anxiety that comes with being a child of a narcissist. It took many years for me to relax and enjoy driving instead of waiting for something bad to happen that would prove my mother right and me incapable.

Another example of narcissistic behaviour was my mother refusing to come to my house. She would send my father to tell me I should go and visit her, but never come to visit me.

This is the control the narcissists crave – I must go to her house, this is where she is in charge. There is no option, no universe where she would not have the upper hand. Her static narcissistic shell would not allow it, because that would put her in danger of narcissistic injury. This attitude is exactly why the narcissists put their children down at any stage of their lives.

At this stage, I knew it in my heart that I should stay away from her. There was simply never a healthy connection between my mother and me. The early childhood dependency and the need for approval were still in my co-dependent mind. This is why she could affect me negatively for so long. That primal, early need for approval and love is hard to override.

SLANDER CAMPAIGNS

An example:

On one of the few occasions I was back at home, I found people were angry with me. I was treated with contempt and disregard by people I had no personal connection with. The only explanation was that my mother had managed to make them dislike me intensely. I do not know what she had told them about me, but it was nothing good.

The reason for her anger was that I finally managed to leave home and get a life. This enrages the narcissistic parent. Getting traction in life gets you further away from the controlled environment the narcissist is happy in, and they will make you pay for it in any way they can. Unfortunately, they know your weak spots and know how to bring you down.

On her part, my narcissistic mother targeted the exact insecurities she had witnessed affecting me badly before – my body issues and the humiliation of being incapable.

My husband was given the credit for any progress in my life, and I was treated with the familiar contempt. My mother was attacking me for not looking after him and for not praising him enough, as if he was superior to me and I had to work hard to keep him or he would certainly discard me. Pointing out I was subservient to him was just an extension of a lifelong campaign of minimisation and destruction of my value as a person.

Another way of achieving that was attacking my physical appearance.

My mother was quite chubby, but that had no relevance to her harsh criticism of my body. When I put on some weight she reacted like a hound sensing blood. My father had a belly too, but he followed my mother's lead and attacked my 'physical appearance' as well. I was within the normal weight measurements according to my doctor, but it was a major issue according to my parents.

I was in my late thirties – some changes in the body are part of life for most people at this age. And yes, demands to stay the same way you were when you were twenty are ridiculous, but it is a part of the static way the dysfunctional narcissistic family exists. You are not allowed to change. And yes, unfortunately, the toxic shame triggered prevents the children of narcissists from seeing how dysfunctional that is.

I felt as devastated by my ugly body as I felt when I was twenty. It was just the way I always felt. It was a weak spot not because I was ever overweight, but because the insecurity was placed so deep into my mind that I managed to feel unattractive in all stages of my life, courtesy of my covert narcissistic mother.

…

This is another example of how static the narcissists are. They will not change, and they will not accept you changing, and they will not change their perception of you.

On one of my rare visits, my mother told me I should start having children because my father had taken a second job and was making good money.

I had my own good job, a husband and a life, but in her head I was still at home and dependent on them. This is how she'd always imagined it, and this was not going to change no matter how my life changed. In her head she was the matriarch who is the head of the family, controls the money, and says what is what. This is the only option she could see as a viable option.

Control is what is important to a covert narcissist. It protects them from injury. She was craving a small child around for supply, and it had nothing to do with me and my decisions. Maybe she was waiting for me to fail at my job and marriage and go back home.

I was hurt because she projected the familiar image of the broken failure who was forever dependent on them. I had to fight that very perception within me every day, and it was a struggle. One visit home brought back all the insecurities I fought to keep at bay.

I told her that at my job I made more money than my father, and it was the truth. She physically recoiled back with the familiar expression – lips tightly shut, chin up, expression of disgust and anger against the universe that allowed her no-good daughter to earn more. She did not say a word. There was no 'well done,' or 'that's nice, dear,' as one would expect a mother to say. Nothing. Just anger at me and anger at the unfairness of this world. Her no-good daughter was successful, and that was not okay.

If you are a child of a narcissist, please understand that you cannot prove yourself or satisfy them. It doesn't matter what you do or achieve. The problem they have with you is not your fault. It is their disorder that drives them. Narcissistic injury is any threat to the false image of the narcissist. It's admitting they are not who they think they are, and they will do anything humanly possible to avoid that.

In her head my mother was always to be the mother, the queen bee, the one that says who is who and what is what. In her expectations the grandchildren were to come under her roof. Without her props of power she probably felt exposed and in danger of narcissistic injury.

Covert narcissists are very brittle; this is why they are more of a nonsense to others than a threat. You, however, their children, they can control and inflict pain on because they had influence on you from birth. They can feed only on the emotionally damaged – people with no self-esteem and no good borders.

You have to accept that you never had a parent that loved you. It had nothing to do with the person you were. You were the main target of someone with a disorder, and there were different rules applied to you than the rest of the world.

If you know that you achieved things, you should be proud of yourself. You know you put your effort into something and you got results. If this is dismissed and your weaknesses are targeted instead, have no doubt: You are a child of a covert narcissist.

What I am trying to convey to you is that talking to a narcissist is not worth it. Whatever you say, they will find a way to twist it and throw something nasty back at you. There cannot be a two-way communication because everything is about them. And they are masters of manipulation – my mother managed to offend me and bring me down even when I was doing well, because this is what she was good at.

Many narcissists treat their grandchildren differently, being easy on them while demeaning their own children. It is a narcissistic twisted game. They might try to take the grandchildren away from the parents if they do not play their part.

The covert narcissists might appear to be vulnerable, but they are vicious. Do not ever underestimate them.

RE-IDEALISING OLD SOURCES OF SUPPLY

After I first left home and went working in a different city, I was completely ignored by my mother. For years she showed no interest in me. The question is why, after you are no longer a supply and they abandon you, they return and try to get back into your life.

One reason is the obvious reason – they want something. When narcissists hit a tough spot and they alienate all their current sources of supply, they will come back to you. The way they justify it in their heads is that you were confused and now you need them more than ever before.

It is called re-idealising of old sources of supply. Suddenly your badness and worthlessness turn into inability and neediness. They have to come to help you because they are such great people, and because they are superior to you.

Do not ever fall for this. Re-idealising old supplies is a sick way of coming back to use you when they have a shortage of supply. Narcissists always want more, this is why they step over borders and even their enablers figure out something is very wrong with the relationship. Of course this is part of the disorder. The two driving forces are need for supply and the fear of narcissistic injury.

This is why when you do well in life it is likely the narcissists will stay away and attack you covertly from a distance. The moment you are weak and in trouble, they will be back.

During my last severe depression, my mother was suddenly friendly and – seconds after seeing me – she was off talking about herself. She had gotten tired of her best friend, and 'everyone had gone crazy,' by which I assume they got fed up with her.

Another reason the narcissist comes back is because they have an agenda. My mother wanted grandchildren. 'Have children soon, so we can help while we can …,' she used to say with a sigh and a face of a long suffering saint, playing the part with a fully fledged dramatic flair.

The narcissistic image demands she must be seen as a devoted wife and mother, presenting herself as a victim, as a long-suffering and always giving and caring person, sacrificing herself for her loved ones. Exactly what the narcissists are not.

NARCISSISTIC TRANSFER

Before I try to explain what narcissistic transfer is, I will give an example.

After a rare visit home I was flying back to work, in a small aeroplane in winter. The weather wasn't good, my mother kept panicking at the airport, going on and on about how worried she was, trying scare tactics till she finally got me worried. She felt the exact moment she got to me and the narcissistic smirk instantly appeared on her face. She was satisfied, or justified, or had met whatever perverted need made her tick.

As a child of a narcissist you have probably felt that moment yourself, when they get to you, affect you negatively, pass their bullshit to you. It makes them smirk, and you know that narcissistic smirk. Even if you had ignored it in the past, you know what it is, you know that expression.

This knowledge can protect you as an adult. Just trust your instincts, and if a person gives away the narcissistic vibe, you move away quickly and quietly. Covert narcissists are hard to spot; they have two faces, and different behaviours in front of people and when they are alone with you. It's part of the abuse strategy.

This is exactly what makes narcissistic abuse unique. Others might not believe you and victimise you all over again. The disbelief messes with your already messed-up head. Nobody will tell a rape victim to try and sort it out with their abuser, but people will gladly tell that to a victim of narcissistic abuse.

These are some of the reasons children of narcissistic parents find it hard to cope, and why with some the co-dependent disorder turns into a life-threatening mental illness. Before I found out about the dynamics of covert narcissistic abuse, I was on the brink of suicide.

REPEATED EPISODES OF DEPRESSION

Because of the damaged sense of self, the erosion of personality, and the lifelong mental issues, the victims are vulnerable to episodes of depression, and each episode tends to be worse than the one before.

An example:

After working hard for years earning money, I thought things would surely improve once I got a home and some financial security. Instead I ended up with another bout of complete exhaustion and the most severe episode of depression and anxiety.

It began with a sense of isolation and social anxiety. In the end, the capabilities of my brain to function were so diminished that everyday tasks became impossible.

I recall finding myself searching for some sort of commune I could go to, something that I would never consider in a better state of mind. It was about being with people who could not live normal lives, like me. I assume people who become members of strange sects and alternative groups feel a similar way, whatever the reasons might be.

Part of the problem was my inability to lean on anybody, not even my husband. I was not talking about the suicidal way I felt, not even admitting how bad it was to the doctor because of the lifetime habit of hiding my feelings.

Everything was an assault on my brain – noises were louder, emotions were sharper, and every little thing could hurt me deeply. Even the wind blowing in my face was trying to get me. All unpleasant, unresolved things stuffed inside, came out. It was an illness that was getting worse because my defences were getting weaker.

This is how the narcissistic abuse becomes self-prophecy. The negative conditioning you grew up with made your life miserable. Misery drained your energy and you ended up unable to cope – exactly what the narcissist was trying to convince you that you were incapable of.

My mother was happy to be back in the game, glowing with pleasure and self-righteousness; I was miserable and I needed her to tell me what was wrong with me. At this very low point of my life she nearly drove me over the edge with attacks on my weight, on my hair, on my medication, on my character.

It was the final revelation – she did not and she never would care about me. She would not make the slightest of efforts to help me get better, but she'd do the exact opposite – push me down even lower.

WHY SUICIDE

Suicide is the last resort when the mental torture gets so bad one cannot stand the pain. Because the pain is not expressed in a physical manner – no visible blood and guts – this is not understood. Mental wounds can get septic and the agony and turmoil in the brain can have the same effect as pain.

An example:

At the peak of my illness I ended up curled up on the kitchen floor and screaming at the top of my lungs. The pain came in waves, like heat waves. It felt like burning in my mind, rising and rising till I screamed and repeated 'go away, please go away.' Luckily, every time the pain subsided.

I think it was a state of depletion and disintegration of the protective layer around my being. It was a result of the constant assaults I was experiencing. Anything felt like an attack, from my husband, shop assistants, friends, neighbours, dogs in the park, wind, noises in the house.

This time there was another new aspect to my state of depression. It was anger, but not the usual anger turned inwards.

I recall standing in front of the local library on a beautiful sunny day, and suddenly not wanting to go in. I was looking around; beautiful people, little children, cute little dogs, and hating them all. I was feeling very resentful and angry that nobody cared about the agony I was in.

This sudden anger and hatred against random people was probably some consequence of my depression, and it made me think about those people that make the news for shooting randomly into a crowd. That experience of hatred and rage scared me, I figured I had to do something about my state of mind and I went to a doctor. The medication he prescribed helped a little, but it was not a solution.

THE POINT OF NO RETURN WITH A NARCISSISTIC PARENT

I was in a world of pain, but the deepest and most painful experiences always came from my childhood. No recent events could compare with the hurt coming from the small child inside, and no pain was more devastating than the one my mother could inflict.

After I saw her glowing with satisfaction because of my miserable state, there was no way back, and some part of me knew what to do. I went no contact before I knew what the concept of no contact was, or what a narcissistic disorder was. It was the logical and the only choice. It was me or her, and I chose me.

My mental health improved after I stopped all contact with my narcissistic mother and her flying monkeys. But the real change came with the understanding of the narcissistic abuse and behaviour and understanding what I needed to do in order to heal.

…

Ironically, around this time my father suffered a psychotic episode. His own problems were getting worse, and he ended up imagining

Russian scientists and invisible heat rays trying to kill him for some reason.

His mental state was probably as bad as mine, but it manifested itself differently. His social anxiety and obsessive-compulsive personality tendencies were getting worse with time.

Narcissists do not contribute in a meaningful way to a relationship and to the well-being of their spouses. My mother was using his dysfunction in a way that was good for her. She used narcissistic techniques against him as well, passing the blame and affecting his judgment, but he could not understand he was being manipulated and could not figure out how his inability to deal with his own emotions made him a puppet.

Amazingly, his problems were forgotten as suddenly both united to fix me and put me back into my place. With me in the picture the family could go back to the old way of focusing on my problems and my shortcomings and taking the attention away from their own.

I suspect that after I left and stopped all communication with them, the problems continued and got worse without a Scapegoat. I also suspect my mother would be the last to unravel, and only if she is left with no one to feed on. Very unfortunately, the narcissists outlast their victims. They are very good at surviving on others.

LESSONS I LEARNED AS AN ADULT

Once more, a covert narcissistic mother would never be the parent you craved for. Understand that and accept it, and give up trying to please her. Instead take charge of your own state of mind.

That feeling of being reduced to a child, feeling helpless, angry, and teary when you are back home, is about going back to an infantile stage of misery and being emotionally overwhelmed by the narcissistic abuse.

Going no contact is the first step to start looking after your well-being and that of your family, if you happen to have one. Personally, I never wanted children. I knew I did not have the healthy mental state to be a good mother. It is a tough gig, and one must have the right reasons and the willingness to raise children.

For that reason, there was nothing for my mother to actively go after. Covert narcissists don't have the confidence of the overt narcissists to openly attack if the incentives are not there. She was no longer present in my life, but the issues she created were still there and needed to be dealt with.

After no contact you have to make your recovery a priority. In order to heal, you first have to understand that the problems did not come from you. The narcissistic personality disorder got transferred into you as a disorder with different parameters. Narcissists have power in the family and condition their children to become co-dependents – people pleasers with no self-esteem.

Abusers of any kind are not well people, and they don't want you to be one either. The abuse is a sign of anger and frustration that must be let go of, and you were the convenient choice. This is why it is so important for us as a society to deal with mental illness. Each victim affects the mental health of the next generation.

PART V: Recovery

You might be wondering why most of this book is about the damage rather than the very important part of the recovery. Going back and understanding what happened is a large and very important part of the recovery. Understanding how and why you experienced your existence the way you did, and the dynamics of narcissistic manipulations, is the beginning of the healing process.

You have to take this journey for yourself, no matter how painful it might be at times. You have to find out where your behaviour patterns came from. Instead of experiencing emotions in an infantile state you'd be able to calm the child you were and take a hold of your reactions and emotions as a grown person.

This journey takes time and effort, but it's worth it. Narcissists are very unlikely to change because they are unable to see how much is wrong with them, but you can change.

STEPS TO RECOVERY

NO CONTACT

In my case, no contact was an easy choice. But if you are a young person there are other things to consider.

Going away physically is not enough and you have to be well enough to make it on your own. There was a time I was not able to get away because of depression and mental breakdowns.

If you are not in a state to cope on your own you need to recover sufficiently first. It is not impossible. Do not rush into anything. For you there are techniques you can you use to minimise the damage of living with a narcissist.

It might be even more beneficial if you can get the narcissists out of your head even when they are next to you. Remember, it is your decency, your guilt, your good nature that feeds them. If you figure out how they manipulate you, you can prevent it and even manipulate them until you can find a healthier and happier way to be.

Learn about those techniques – for example, the 'observe, do not absorb,' and the 'grey stone' technique.

Learn as much as you can about the disorder. Do not directly challenge the narcissistic parent with what you've learned. It's pointless, and it's dangerous at this stage. Resist the urge, though you might experience strong feelings of anger and hurt. Remember your target is to get better. Recovery should be your goal, not taking the narcissist down.

Once you know more by using the 'observe, do not absorb' technique, you can see through the manipulation and remain unaffected. Start understanding the reasons they behave the way they do and why you react to them the way you do.

'Grey stone' is about not feeding the narcissist with your emotions. Do not provoke them, though they will try to get the best out of you as you get better.

Do what one should do to get away from any abuser when exhausted and mentally unfit – make a realistic plan of escape, or you might make matters worse. In the meantime, keep on learning about narcissism and about techniques to improve your mental health. Do not try to explain to the flying monkeys what the narcissists are. It is your first goal to help yourself, and once you are healthy you can help others.

IF YOU ARE AN ADULT CHILD OF A NARCISSIST

If you are an adult child of a narcissist, then there is no question: go no contact. Do not try to explain anything to them, just get out. You have your own life, cut any contact and stay away from your dysfunctional family of origin. Nothing is worth the mental destruction they cause. They will end up worse off, and you have everything to gain.

The point I am trying to make is that if you are unable to relax when you are with your family of origin, if you feel miserable because of them, then you don't have to stay. You've been conditioned not to believe your feelings. But if you feel bad when you are with certain people, they are not good for you. If you can avoid it, do not force yourself to be near them out of any false sense of duty or fear.

I cannot repeat it enough: do not explain yourself to the narcissistic parent. There is no point of getting into any verbal arguments. They flourish in it, and you will suffer. Don't fight them directly. They will play the victim, and they are expert manipulators able to feed on any attention, as long as they are in some way still involved in your life.

As long as they have an access they will feed on your emotions. If you have to talk to them, stay distant and do not give them information about yourself. Just say you do not wish to have any contact with them, and that's that.

A win against a narcissist is living a good life.

You have to learn to stick with your truth whether others believe you or not. Covert narcissists are not obvious to most people. Start the healing process and work on a new way of thinking and feeling about yourself.

You are going to meet other narcissists, do not let them in your life. And if you do, you have to employ the 'grey stone' and the 'observe but do not absorb' techniques, and try to get rid of them.

Most importantly, forgive yourself for any mistakes you have made in the past. You survived, and you were under attack ever since you were born. It takes someone with ability, sense, and intuition. Embrace who you are, even when you feel fragile and exhausted.

Forgiveness is often used in a religious sense – forgive those who have wronged you. This is not what I mean. Victims of narcissistic abuse tend to punish themselves for being stupid and not figuring out sooner what the narcissistic game was. This is just a repeat of a bad pattern of thinking. It was never your fault, but forgiving is about letting go and moving on. Embrace and respect yourself.

DO NOT BELIEVE NARCISSISTS WILL CHANGE

Once you get away, the narcissistic parent will try to get you back with all sorts of pretences. Don't fall for it, not again. Your toxic family has roles, and everything they do is to push you back into the Scapegoat role. Do not give them any information about yourself and do not try to explain anything.

OTHER THINGS TO KNOW ABOUT NO CONTACT

As I mentioned before, physically getting away from the narcissists will not heal you alone. No matter how far you go, their poison is inside you. It is just the first step, then you have to go through a healing process. If you come from a narcissistic family you have to rethink the entire value system instilled in you and stop feeling inferior.

And as you break free from the narcissistic illusion and your dysfunctional family, you will experience a lot of hatred coming at you from the narcissistic parent and their flying monkeys. And you will be unfairly judged by people not close enough to know what the real story is. You have to get through it and learn to stay with your truth.

Yes, I know how deep the childhood desire to please is. But think about it: If you are liked by a narcissist, you have to worry. If they hate you, it's because you are doing well and you are no longer playing their sick games.

The same is true of the flying monkeys: they are not worth your time. Move on. Even from close relatives - it is not your job to save them from the narcissist. First of all you have to save yourself.

You have to accept that not all people are good, and not all mothers are good. Most are, and mothers are very important, and this is why the few unlucky ones have to deal with a world of pain.

BEGINNING THE HEALING PROCESS

There are things to keep in mind and things to avoid.

Going back to the earliest memories and reviewing them is a good place to start. It's where your brain will not want to go to at first, but it is a necessary part of the process.

Once you start understanding the damage the childhood abuse did, you are going to feel an overwhelming anger. Be angry, but do not act on it. You will not be in a state to make sound decisions about what to do. Remember, your anger will subside with time.

Do not be afraid to feel your emotions, as long as they don't control you. Be honest and try to verbalise what you feel, because you've been made to ignore your senses and your needs. When you experience overwhelming feelings, put your hand on your chest and say aloud how you feel. This works for anger, and for any other strong emotion. Just saying what you feel reduces it by half.

You have to go through a grieving process, grieving the loss of time and the loss of the hope that you will ever have good, supportive parents. Go through the stages without holding back, till you are ready to let go.

Don't break no contact. Learn techniques to improve your daily life and to combat stress and Complex PTSD.

Love yourself unconditionally, because you are going to make the old mistakes a few more times. It's easy to fall into the old pattern of behaviour when you are stressed and tired. Be very kind and patient with yourself when you do, try to calm the little child inside. Your reactions to your mistakes will make the real difference in time.

As a rule, do not try to explain to people who have never experienced narcissistic abuse. They have to experience it, or be very fine-tuned emotionally, to understand your pain. Other empaths, or people with similar experiences, will understand, and finding a community online to share with is the best thing you can do.

Someone who has never been a victim and is reading this might say that the narcissists are as much victims as the people they destroy, because they had some sort of abnormal childhood. They are entitled to their opinion, but not to telling you how to handle your situation.

If you are a victim of a narcissistic parent, for you and me, there are different rules. Do not ever feel sorry for a narcissist. We have our own disorder, and it makes us a prey for predatory types and users. We are who they are after, because the narcissists cannot take from a normal person as much as they can from us.

HOW TO HANDLE THE INNER CRITIC

The inner critic is the criticising voice inside your head shaped by the attitude of the narcissistic parent. Once you understand how damaging it is you can change it by catching it as it tries to put you down and consciously changing the message to a positive and caring one.

Be patient. The inner voice was formed in your juvenile years and came with the narcissistic inbuilt position of control. It is formed with the toxic shame to work against you for the benefit of the parent.

To get into the habit and develop a positive inner voice, you have to practice saying positive things to yourself. Develop a mantra that works for you and repeat it when you get stressed.

Try to learn to love all those flaws you used to punish yourself for, love your body as it is. It will take time, but once you manage to shift your mindset you will experience enormous relief and a sense of freedom.

EMOTIONAL FLASHBACKS

You might have never heard of emotional flashbacks, but as a child of a narcissist you are more than likely to have experienced them.

Those are flashbacks of shaming and humiliating moments of your past. They can pop up in your head at any time and make your mind re-experience them. From embarrassing moments at school, to traffic mishaps, to social blunders. All those times you failed to perform are coming back in a flash, and that does nothing but feed the toxic shame.

It is something the old part of the brain does, and it's looking for danger. This is why it keeps on replaying those moments you found so distressing again and again.

When you have an emotional flashback, the muscles contract, the breathing becomes shallow, the heart beats faster, and it feels like a sharp burn in the mind and makes you flinch and retreat both mentally and physically.

Some memories are stored in a childlike state, as they were experienced. Others trigger the state of toxic shame that is imbedded in the people-pleaser's mind. Being humiliated is registered as danger in your mind, because it was in the narcissistic family.

DEALING WITH EMOTIONAL FLASHBACKS

To combat their effect, learn to recognise emotional flashbacks and acknowledge that you are having a flashback.

Then take a deep breath and bring yourself to the present. Say 'I am having a flashback' aloud if you need to. Put your hand on your chest. Remember you are safe and well now, and that you have a choice how to feel. Those flashbacks are useless and harmful, and they are the result of dysfunction and self-hatred.

Relax your body and be very compassionate to yourself. Consciously examine where it came from, and try to point to the underlying issues triggering the wave of toxic shame.

Without the toxic shame, the flashbacks are just human experiences, and everybody has experiences like that. You are not supposed to be perfect or better than everyone to matter, this was the poison of the narcissistic abuser who shamed you out of your mind. Be compassionate and very nice to yourself.

Eventually, you will move your reaction to the frontal lobe, rethink the danger and react with reason rather than with emotion and fear.

HOW TO COMBAT TOXIC SHAME

The cure for toxic shame is compassion and acceptance. This is what was missing from your upbringing and from your way of thinking.

As I mentioned before, people who are able to admit their faults and embrace their human true self are stronger, happier, and more capable. Toxic shame paralyses the mind and the body, it was a weapon used on you in your dysfunctional family of origin.

You have to get through, and to the other side. If you recoil and contract internally every time the shame is triggered, it will not go away. Embrace your past; do not try to run from it. Remember, you already have all the worth and value you will ever need, it comes with being alive. If you embrace it, nobody can take it away.

Acceptance is a necessary part of the recovery. Accept that you are human and that whatever happened to you happened to you, this is just a part of life. Your shortcomings do not make you bad. They make you human. You were never bad – the narcissistic parents made you think that.

They will never admit to any wrongdoings, so do not expect an apology or any meaningful gesture on their side to make you feel better. With time the narcissists get worse, it's the only way their separation from reality can end up.

DO NOT TRY TO HELP OTHERS IF YOU ARE SICK

Another important thing to remember is that during your recovery you are still vulnerable and have to take extra care. First, you have to fight your fight, because if you are not well you cannot help others and have to be looked after.

If other members of your family you care for are siding with the abuser, you have to leave them behind and move on. I am sorry, but you have to choose between your sanity and the narcissistic poison.

NOTICE THE AFTERMATH OF THE NARCISSISTIC ABUSE

Learn what the signs of narcissistic abuse are, how they affect you and how to combat them. Your default settings are so far from normal that it is hard for you to understand what a normal existence is like.

Like breathing, for example. Believe it or not, you have to learn how to breathe. Notice when you are holding your breath, it is not a normal thing. Shallow breathing is a sign of constant stress. You are more likely to suffer panic attacks and emotional irregularity if you do not breathe properly.

Notice if your muscles tighten almost immediately after you wake up. It is a learned response to a false reality. High alert has become your normal state, and it has been for many years. This is why I cannot repeat enough: be kind to yourself, because those who were supposed to were not.

Both breathing and muscle tension are signs of Complex PTSD. Learn more about it, the signs and the triggers behind it. Even if you say to yourself, 'I know what this is,' it will take the edge off.

Notice when people are trying to use you and speak up. If they move away because of it, they are not the people you want in your life.

Notice why you want to do things, such as changing your habits, clothes, or furniture; is it because it's you, or because you are comparing yourself to someone, or because you are trying to please someone.

Notice why you feel offended by someone – is it their design to offend you or are you overreacting because you have low self-esteem and assume you are always a target. People have issues of their own, and their own insecurities.

Notice when you are slipping into a familiar state of tension. Notice when you need time out. Notice why you eat, for example; is it because you are hungry or because you are trying to improve your state of mind.

Basically, use your frontal lobe, reasoning and logic, to figure out where the pressure comes from – from a real danger, or from the Complex PTSD.

As a good rule, do not waste energy on things that are not important to your survival and mental health improvement.

INTIMACY ISSUES AND RECOVERY

Keep in mind that not knowing what a good relationship should be like, is messing with your life. It's common for children of narcissists to become overwhelmed by their partner's troubles and make them their own, as well as putting their wishes aside to accommodate the partner's and eventually ending up resentful. It is a consequence of the lack of borders and it is not good for the relationship.

Ironically, the more loving and caring a partner is, the more tension is created. It is a twist very much unique to narcissistic abuse.

Another thing to watch out for is getting irritated when your partner expresses loving feelings, because the suspended misbelief is triggered. You might be tempted to challenge that verbally or in your head and sabotage the relationship.

This is why many co-dependents marry narcissists, and the cycle of abuse continues. Familiarity is a comfort to those who are in a state of tension and distress, because it justifies their experiences.

PICKING UP NARCISSISTIC TRAITS OF YOUR OWN

Thinking that everything people say or do has something to do with you, is one trait that is similar to the narcissistic behaviour. Being so tender inside from the abuse makes you constantly look for people attacking you in some way.

People do and say things because of a number of reasons, that is just the way it is, and they should not affect you the way they do. If they do, it's because you lack good boundaries and a sense of strong self.

Ironically, what you have picked up from the narcissistic abuser is the need to be validated by outside sources. You have to learn how to validate yourself.

Try not to read too much into what people say, or care much what they think. People come and go; you should be the main character in your life.

WHAT TO CONCENTRATE ON

The most important thing is to change how you think and how you feel about yourself.

You have to learn to treat yourself differently, to stop pressuring and harassing yourself as your parents did, and be respectful and good to yourself.

Your sense of self was never wiped completely because you managed to see through the narcissistic manipulation even when you didn't know how to deal with it. Trust your senses, that wise part of you.

WHAT GOOD MENTAL HEALTH IS

Good mental health is having healthy self-esteem, the ability to communicate efficiently, having positive relationships, enjoying activities, and coping with problems and with changes as they come. It is about achieving your potential and living a full life. Knowing your value is beyond what you do or how much you have. It is a big world and you have the same right to be as anyone and everyone.

Strong, secure people do not worry about their weaknesses, and it's not because they don't have them. Strength is in accepting you have weaknesses and strong points and dealing with both in a helpful and appropriate manner. This way you make the best out of what you are given.

Victims of narcissistic abuse have been raised with the opposite of good mental health. In the toxic family atmosphere, you developed a mental illness of your own. The long-term stress, long-term pattern of negative thoughts, and low self-esteem, affected and distorted your perceptions.

I suffered inside for my perceived weaknesses and punished myself constantly throughout my life. This is the programming I was raised with. Once I understood what I was doing wrong I managed to gradually reduce the amount of self-abuse and improve my life.

WHY MENTAL HEALTH IS STILL A 'DIRTY SECRET'

Taking care of yourself and your mental health is still not talked about openly. It feels like the topic of personal well-being is a dirty secret because society does not want self-absorbed people.

You, however, are the very opposite. You need self-love, this is what is missing. You need healthy narcissism. Being mentally healthy has nothing to do with being a narcissist.

It is not wrong to care for yourself. If you are healthy, you can help others. Prioritise your rest and sleep as needed, over the demands of others. If you don't, you will fall apart and become a burden. Yes, work to be the best version of yourself, improve on the things you think you should improve on. But do learn to treat yourself with respect and care. You must accept what you cannot fix, and improve what you can in a constructive and helpful way.

You should be comfortable in your skin, because that's who you are every second of your life. Being your own enemy is a no-win situation.

This is a very basic concept, yet many adult children of narcissistic parents spend years in self-loathing and distorted perception. Unlike the false narcissistic image, their 'bad' image can improve and children of narcissists can find their way out of the dysfunction.

DO NOT COMPARE YOURSELF TO OTHERS

As an adult child of a narcissist you are facing problems the majority of people around you are not. Do not compare yourself to anyone else, because you are not like anyone else. The target for you is to regain the feeling of normality and self-sufficiency, anything else can only come after it.

There will be a period of time during your recovery when your state of mind will improve, and yet your brain and body will react the same old way they are conditioned to. For example, social situations that no longer scare you might still evoke the same shaky voice and inability to communicate. Do not worry about it; it is a stage of the recovery, and an important one at that.

The key to recovery is to accept your old reactions without attacking yourself for it, without being angry or negative, no matter how much you repeat old mistakes and behaviour. Be compassionate and kind instead, and carry on with your recovery process. This new attitude will finally change the reaction of the 'old brain.'

People might still think you are weird, or slow, but that does not matter. If you worry about that, you've missed the point. The point is that you should not care whether some people think you are weird or not. Yes, I know, it is a hard concept for adult children of narcissists to comprehend. A vital piece was taken away, the self-love and the self-preservation that allows others to thrive. Once you regain that, you will be okay.

Another thing you should watch for is what kind of people you let into your life. During my last depression episode I noticed that many people were cautious of me. They probably sensed I had some issues being a functioning human being, and took a step back. Yet people with predatory traits saw me coming from miles off and stuck to me like glue because they sensed they could take advantage of me. I managed to eventually detach myself from those people.

You have to learn what works for you and what does not, to get to know yourself and be honest about your strengths and weaknesses. For example, I get tired easily, my body and mind cannot cope with what most people can, and I have accepted that. The way to manage that is to prioritise sleep and not to overstretch doing things that are not important.

Whatever your weaknesses, just do what you consider is best for you, and do not try to be different because someone disapproves of you.

Basically, what I am trying to say is that looking after yourself is not selfish. It is essential.

Of course you can go the other way and care for nobody but yourself, and that would not be good. But if you are a child of a narcissist it would be very unlikely that you will stop being empathic altogether.

TIPS FOR DEALING WITH PEOPLE WHILE IN RECOVERY

Part of the recovery process is about breaking the old people-pleasing habits. Below are some rules to help you deal with exploitative personality types.

If someone is asking for a favour, do not be pressured into saying yes or no to anything immediately. If you don't feel comfortable, take some time and think about what you want. Just say, 'I will think about it and let you know,' or 'I need some time, thank you.' Or just say 'No, I have plans,' you don't have to explain yourself.

Watch out for being pulled into other people's agendas, to take care of their well-being while you need help yourself. It is about falling back into old patterns without even realising it. As an empath, you might have the urge to help, whether it's feasible or not. Resist that urge. Becoming your own person is about making things happen instead of reacting to what others want.

If you suspect someone is a narcissist, speak cheerful phrases that mean nothing and move away. Don't give any details of your life, do not share emotions. Say everything is fine and you have things to do; end of story.

Do not let anyone pressure you into socialising when you don't feel like it. Don't compare yourself to those with non-abusive family history. Try to feel better every day, this is progress and not what someone without a clue about abuse thinks.

Embrace your faults; this is what will set you apart from the narcissists. Practice positive thinking, self-championing, self-soothing. You have to change the programming you were raised with.

Sometimes you just have to remove yourself from a situation that makes you feel uncomfortable. Adult children of narcissists tend to freeze instead of taking action, but you have to learn to do what is good for you.

If negativity affects you badly, avoid negative people and situations, negative news, movies, or TV shows.

Speak your mind; don't just say what others want you to. Agree to disagree; you don't have to defend your opinion. You have to stop being a support character for others and become the leading person in your own life. That means putting your agenda first.

WHAT I FOUND DIFFICULT ON THE WAY TO RECOVERY

On occasion, I kept on reverting to my old state of irrational anxiety; it kept on happening even after my mother was out of my life for good. For example, once I went for an appointment on the wrong date and suddenly I felt I was that stupid person I hated again. This simple mistake should've caused no more than slight irritation for the time wasted getting there and back. Instead I was attacking myself once again.

At this stage, I understood the damage that was done yet I kept on reverting to the old fear of adding another flashback, another painful memory. I was going back to the tension, to tightening my muscles, clenching my hands and my jaw. This state of anxiety and self-hatred was imprinted on my brain from a very early age and appeared to be very hard to override.

WHAT WORKED FOR ME

The strategy I finally found working for this type of anxiety was similar to the one working for panic attacks. It might seem counterintuitive, but so is the tendency to self-destroy. Self-preservation should be the default, not self-destruction.

The technique is as follows: Instead of pulling away and trying to ignore or somehow override the negative feelings, do the opposite – experience the full-blown feeling of hurt, or disappointment, or pain. Whatever it is, experience it fully, embrace it.

First, take a moment, take a breath, relax, and let the feeling be. Gently and patiently examine and observe the feeling, where it comes from, how it feels in your chest, in your shoulders and under the ribcage.

Whatever it is – pain, annoyance, embarrassment – just experience it for as long as you can. Put your hand on your chest and say how you feel. Experience it without flinching away, because as long as you flinch the feeling will keep a hold of you. Let the feeling be for as long as it takes, then let go.

Then engage reason and logic, and everything you've learned. Experience empathy and compassion for yourself and for the damage done to you by the prolonged abuse you had to endure. Feel self-love and understand nothing can get you down if you are authentic and not afraid to feel or fail.

After a while, you will find that the feeling is gone completely. You experienced it genuinely, and that is what it takes to move on. Experiencing authentic feelings is very cathartic.

EXPERIENCING AUTHENTIC FEELINGS

The very action of pulling away, avoiding, hiding, trying to ignore negative emotions, is why they have such power over you.

The emotional flashbacks, for example; if they keep on coming you will be tempted to get angry with yourself. Do not. Each time you flinch, or cover your face in disgrace, you let it take hold of you. Instead let the feeling be, stop and observe it. Ask yourself why this is happening and what use is it. This will engage the frontal lobe, the reason and logic. Then exercise compassion and care, and feel all good and comforting things about yourself.

The damage you are repairing is the way the narcissistic parent made you hide any negative feelings you had. Your default reaction is to back away, to be ashamed and hide. This is why they remain unresolved and clutter your mind.

WHAT HAPPENS TO THE NARCISSISTS

As they get older, narcissists are not likely to get better, only worse – they use others, burn bridges, and sooner or later show their true colours. No matter how much supply they get, they always want more.

With time, covert narcissists start to slip up more and more, become more aggressive as their false image clashes with their actual lives, but still cannot get the level of external validation they need. Eventually, they alienate most people around them and the narcissistic supply dries up.

Narcissists are likely to end their days in misery because the 'feeling good' does not come from the inside, and their ability to hide their predatory ways wears off.

If they are desperate enough, they might come back to those they had previously discarded, and put on a show, playing their last card – acting all pathetic and vulnerable to get you back.

Do not fall for it. Narcissists use your morals, but they do not have any. In their heads they had come up with some fabricated justification that you need them more, and will try to take you down as soon as they get the chance. It is who they are.

Once you manage to get away, stay away. This is my advice. Take their hatred as a good thing. Being hated means you are not a good 'meal.' You've seen through, blown their cover, challenged them. It means you are no longer a co-dependent and you are on the way to recovery.

Do not try to take revenge and do not worry about the narcissists getting what they deserve. Yes, I know it's hard to let go of the hurt and the anger. Yet revenge is not what you should do. Narcissists are pure poison and as long you engage with them you will be exposed to that poison. As long as you interact with them in some way, they will manage to feed on the attention, even if the attention is negative. They will claim the status of the suffering victim without any regard for the reality.

The best thing to do is give them nothing. It's time to put yourself first now and break the chains of bad mental health as far as you are concerned.

Asking why this happened to you is pointless. There is no answer. Many things in life are down to chance. Unfortunately, you were not allowed to grow and thrive in the dysfunctional narcissistic family, and that was not your fault. There is serious damage done to you over the years, but it can be undone.

You are going to heal. It might take time, but one day you will be fine, no longer angry or hurt, and no longer thinking about what happened to you every single day. You will be able to enjoy the small things and have a good life.

SEEING YOUR PARENTS IN A NEW WAY

Part of the recovery process is being able to see your parents for the people they are, not as parents. It will make their power over you disappear.

In perspective, my parents were angry with their parents, disappointed by their children, unhappy with the political system and with the society in general that somehow failed to listen and do what they say. Their way of life was complaining and criticising and never taking responsibility for their behaviour. They were simply not the good kind of people.

The only power they had was in the family, and they took their frustrations out on their children, demeaning and demanding respect without earning it, expecting rewards without putting any effort into it.

Such people, parents or not, do not deserve a second of your time.

HOW TO MAINTAIN GOOD MENTAL HEALTH

Have you ever felt that if life was a race then you were kept way back and everyone is now far in the distance? It is lonely, hopeless, and humiliating being left so far behind.

This perception is at the heart of the misery many victims of narcissistic abuse experience. There is no race; comparing yourself with others and finding you are lacking is just that – an unhealthy perception.

Happiness is a state of mind, and it's not measured with money or status. There will always be better people, more clever, more rich or beautiful, or talented, or whatever you decide to look for. It is a fact.

You do not need to be the best to have self-esteem and live well. This is what the narcissist did to you, destroyed the matter and value that naturally comes with being alive. This is what was done to you at a very early age, and what you suffered from ever since.

WHAT RECOVERY IS AND HOW IT FEELS

You will know when you get that uplifting feeling of warmth, of being at peace and being loved. It can be described as high spirits, a sort of natural high that comes with being healthy and well. You might've experienced it at some period of your life, but you might've forgotten how that felt. The source is in your brain, of course, but it feels inside your chest, forehead, and nasal passages, same as toxic shame, but it is the very opposite experience.

This is what you are going for – a good vibe inside of you, being in a good place when you wake up, have a cup of tea, when you wait at a bus stop or when you are stuck in traffic. Being in a good place is feeling good and thinking well of yourself. It helps you make good decisions and experience your existence from your point of view. Being in a good place inside means you can get what you need and give back in return.

This is the goal. Once you manage to get in that state – feeling positivity and self-assurance most of the time – your perception will shift and the illusion of the race will cease to bother you or to be of any importance.

You will get to that point by accepting that you are who you are with all your strengths and flaws. You do not have to be superior to others to like and respect who you are and to enjoy your life.

SUMMARY OF RECOVERY

You are not going to miraculously wake up the next day and be perfectly alright. But you will be one day. Every little effort you make will pay off in the future, the same way each put-down dragged you down in the past. Once you get to enjoy the small things you will find that's more than sufficient. It's about the small things, and amazingly this is the big secret of sanity.

It will happen gradually, and one day you will notice a change. After that you might experience a relapse, or you might not, but in time you will find a major shift has happened and you are on solid ground. It's a great feeling.

Some of you might be wondering what gives me the right to tell others how to recover, and whether I have recovered from the narcissistic abuse and all the related mental health issues.

Well, maybe not all of them, but as I stated above I believe I am a survivor of narcissistic abuse. I no longer experience life as a victim. The next stage is thriving and hopefully I will get there in time.

To me, recovery feels like having a positive state of mind more often than not, and having that feeling of lightness and enjoyment that makes doing things easier and enjoyable.

I do still get the occasional flashback, but I know how to handle it. Of course I still experience deep sadness when I think about all the years wasted, but it's a feeling of sadness and not depression. I do not feel isolated, but I enjoy being alone very much. I do not feel I am less than anyone, and I do not have the need to be better than anyone.

Recovering is a process, the same way the damage inflicted by the abuse was a process, and recovery is very likely if you follow through.

WHY I WROTE THIS BOOK

My recovery started when I stumbled onto information about covert narcissists online while I was researching ways to recover from depression. The information resonated very much with my life experiences. After that I started reading everything I could find on the topic.

Then I learned about emotional abuse and the effect it has on children, and a lot of what was wrong with me was explained. I was no longer alone and confused, because there were many people experiencing the exact same thing I was.

We all know what the chain of violence is, but the same principle can be applied to helping people instead of hurting them.

I received help and I appreciate that very much. I'd like to return it and tell anyone who needs help to keep on looking for answers. Even if this book does not fit your personality, temperament, or experience, please keep on searching. Knowledge is about looking for answers, and you will know it when you find something helpful.

I want to thank everyone who spoke and wrote about their struggles. Getting narcissistic abuse out in the open is a good thing. The less prey they can get their hands on, the less damage they will do.

There are a variety of sources online, bloggers, websites, and articles. Find out what works for you and answers your questions.

Below are the names of good academic sources I used for my recovery:

Pete Walker
Ross A. Rosenberg
Karyl McBride
Jonice Webb
Pea Mellody
Gail Meyers
Beverly Engel

Excellent YouTube channels:

Spartan life coach
Understanding Narcissists
Peace and Harmony
From Surviving To Thriving
SelfLoveU
Inner Integration

And many others. There are a variety of sources, bloggers, websites, and articles. Find out what works for you and answers your questions.

Printed in Great
Britain
by Amazon